Countdown
to
College

COUNTDOWN TO COLLEGE

A Student's Guide to Getting the Most Out of High School

Zola Dincin Schneider

Phyllis B. Kalb

COLLEGE ENTRANCE EXAMINATION BOARD, NEW YORK

Copies of this book are available from your local bookseller or may be ordered from College Board Publications, Box 886, New York, New York 10101.

Editorial inquiries concerning this book should be directed to Editorial Office, The College Board, 45 Columbus Avenue, New York, New York 10023–6992.

Library of Congress Catalog Number: 89–061953

ISBN: 0–87447–335 –7

Printed in the United States of America

For Erasmus Hall High School
and
Harry Wedeck and Ellis Johnson
two teachers who helped me make the most of it
Z.D.S.

For Sue, Dorothy, and Jack
supporters and inspirers
before, during, and after high school
P.B.K.

Contents

Acknowledgments   xiii

Introduction   1

1

Taking Charge   5

Steering Your Way   7
The Big Question   8
On Your Mark   8
The Choice Is Yours   9

2

Scheduling a Balanced Academic Program   11

Don't Miss Out on the Basics   13
What Are the Basics?   14
Beyond the Basics   14
Quality and Content Count   15
Finding Outstanding Courses   16
Making Decisions about Advanced Courses   16
     Higher Functions?   17
     Scientific Connections   18
     Parlez-Vous, Sprechen Sie, Habla Usted?   18
Why Bother with a Heavy Schedule?   19
Scheduling Your Program   19
For Your Information   20

Tackling the Big Skills: Reading, Writing, Speaking 21

Discovering Books   23
The Rewards of Reading   24
TV and Movies Aren't the Answer   24
Open Bookshelves   25
Browsing   26
Book Reviews   26
Finding Time for Reading   27
Putting Ideas into Words   28
    Practice Writing   29
    Speak Out   30
    Speak Up   30
    Ask the Right Questions   31
For Your Information   33

Organizing Time and Space 35

What Time Is It?   37
Time Wasters   38
Taking Account of Your Time   40
Time for a Change   41
Are You a Procrastinator?   43
Why Do You Procrastinate?   45
Stopping the Habit   46
Easing Parental Pressure   46
Where Did You Put It? Organizing Your
    Work Area   47
Organizing Your Notebook and Assignments   48
Lifetime Skills   49
For Your Information   49

What Do You Hear? What Do You Know? Listening, Taking Notes, Studying 51

What Is Listening? 53
The Problem of Boredom 54
Cures for Boredom 55
Avoiding Distractions 56
Listening with Pencil and Paper 57
   Taking Notes in Class 57
   Reviewing Your Notes 59
Tackling the Text 59
The S Q 3R Method 60
For Your Information 62

Academic Troubleshooting 63

Three Students Who Needed Help 65
   Wayne: Getting on Track 65
   Elizabeth: Losing Interest 66
   Darrell: Catching Up 66
People Who Can Help 67
How to Benefit from a Conference 69
Don't Give Up 69

Taking on Greater Academic Challenges 71

Honors Courses 74
Advanced Placement (AP) Courses 74
   Practical Rewards 74
   What College Admissions Counselors Say about AP 75
   Should You Take an AP Course? 75

Contents

The International Baccalaureate 77
When Your High School Has No Advanced Program 77
Internships, Independent Study, and Other Possibilities 78
Developing Special Talents 79
Challenging Yourself 79
For Your Information 80

8

Help! I Need Somebody!
Coping with Special Problems   81

Moving to a New School 83
   Leaving 84
   Settling In 85
Having to Work 86
Family Problems 87
Look to People for Help 88
Other Places to Look for Help 89
   Library Resources 89
   Hotlines 90
You *Can* Do Something about Your Problem 90
For Your Information 91

9

Beyond the Classroom: Participating in
Extracurricular Activities   93

Emma's Choice: A Dramatic Situation 95
Laurie and Bruce: Newspaper Duo 95
Carl: Time Out for Soccer 96
Extracurricular Dividends 96
Don't Take On Too Much 97
Simon: Too Many Activities 97
Nancy: Joining for the Wrong Reasons 97
Tony: Getting Carried Away with One Activity 98
Volunteer Work 99

Paid Part-Time Work 100
Is This Job Necessary? 101
Earning Alternatives 102
An Enriching Experience 102
For Your Information 104

10

Using Summers for Earning and Learning 105

An Ideal Time 107
Dreams of Summer 108
Designing Your Own Summer 108
Ways to Make Wishes Come True 110
Practical Considerations 111
A Flexible Approach Pays Off 112
Planning: The Key to Summer Success 112
Looking Forward to Summer 114
For Your Information 115

11

Putting College in Perspective 117

Why Go to College? 119
Seven Wrong Reasons for Counting College Out 120
Taking Time Out before College 122
Perspective on Your College Options 124
Ten Questions to Help You Put College in Perspective 125
Pressure from Parents 126
For Your Information 127

12

From Now On . . . 131

Index 135

Acknowledgments

One of the pleasures of writing this book was that it gave us the chance to talk to so many people closely involved in education. It was heartening for us to confirm that a point we emphasized to students—that people are willing and eager to help if you ask—was abundantly true. Everyone we approached—high school and college students, teachers and counselors, educators and administrators—generously shared their experiences and insights with us.

The many high school students whom we have counseled over the years on their plans for college were the inspiration for this book. Their experiences, with names changed, are represented throughout. Our students told us of their concerns, difficulties, and hang-ups, as well as their triumphs. They let us know what they thought would help them and other students to make the most of the high school years.

As we followed them to college, they told us what had been missing in their high school preparation and what they had found especially useful. They were thoughtful and frank in indicating what they would change if they had it to do over again.

We want to give special thanks to those students who read and commented on parts of this book in manuscript form: Julie Fanburg, Jesse Marmon, Margaret Crandall, Andrew Warner, and Brendon Rich. We are indebted to Eric Namrow and to our many other students now in college who graciously responded to a questionnaire asking for their reflections: Andrew Billig, Belinda R. Blum, David Boris, Nicole DeGioia, Kiyo Doniger, Elizabeth Dranitzke, Ulrike Drees, Michael Durr, Meg Elliott,

Julia Finn, Emily Freeman, Ted Freeman, Jason Gaarder, Ellen Goodman, Shela Halper, Michael Hartman, Kirsten Hendrickson, David B. Hinchman, Lisa Jaycox, Jim Knopf, Joni Lane, Shannon Lane, Cate Martin, Dave Martin, Marcie Peternick, Jon Secrest, Elizabeth Smith, Charles Tolchin, and Julie Valentine.

College admissions people we consulted contributed their views on such issues as current admission standards, the value of AP and honors courses, work, and extracurricular activities. We especially thank: Wallace Ann Ayres (Swarthmore), Shannon M. Banks (Bates), Gary L. Beatty (James Madison), Parker Beveridge (Colby), Leon M. Braswell (Bowdoin), Jane M. Custeau (University of New Hampshire), Margit Dahl (Yale), Ann K. Fleming (Union), Martha D. Greene (Wake Forest), Beth Gunbrandsen (Santa Fe), Marlyn McGrath Lewis (Harvard), Lydia K. Lisner (University of Richmond), Cheryl A. Nieczkowski (Syracuse), Kenneth Nourse (Union), Rich Plotkin (Vanderbilt), William M. Shain (Macalester), Larry West (Guilford), Carol Del Propost Wheatley (Wooster), Sue Wileman (University of Arizona), Hubbell Wilson (Sweet Briar), and Henry Witman (Carleton).

In the course of preparing this book, we spoke to many teachers, counselors, educational consultants, and guidance personnel. We want to express our special appreciation to Carol L. Reinsberg, Davi Walders, Shirley Levin, Robert Donaldson, Enid Gershen, and Ann M. Reiss for their valuable suggestions.

We are grateful also for the contributions of Robert A. Hochstein of the Carnegie Foundation for the Advancement of Teaching, William C. Parrish of the National Association of Secondary School Principals, and Norman Brandt of the Education Information Branch, U.S. Department of Education.

Carolyn Trager, our editor at the College Board, merits our heartfelt thanks for her expert advice and sustenance from beginning to end.

In-house advisers served as helpful consultants and refreshing critics. Irving Schneider is our most important "without whom . . ." He bravely pushed, pulled, cajoled, commented, analyzed, and reviewed throughout the writing process. We heartily thank Linda Kanefield for her careful reading and thoughtful comments; Norman Schneider for his time and expertise in myriad matters; and Leslie Reagan, Daniel Schneider, and Peter Schneider, who each offered constructive and practical suggestions all along the way. We warmly appreciate the patience, encouragement, and pointed editorial comments of Bernard Kalb. Tanah, Claudia, and Sarinah Kalb, Marina Kalb Duboc, and Samuel Duboc contributed experiences, comments, and advice that added special spice to our narrative.

To all, our many thanks.

Z.D.S.
P.B.K.
Chevy Chase, Maryland
May 1989

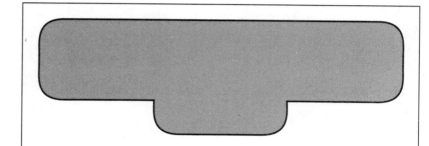

Introduction

I s it possible to tell you, the student, what to do to get the most out of high school?

There are more than 16,000 public schools, and a host of private, parochial, and independent schools, in this country. They vary in size, location, facilities. Funding and control differ; teachers' salaries differ; standards of excellence differ. Students from the many regions—from cities and towns and rural communities—differ.

Within the school itself, there is no way of standardizing students. You come in all shapes and sizes, all degrees of social, academic, athletic interest and ability. Some of you know from the start that you are bound for college—the only question is: which one? Some of you come from families in which no one has gone to college; you hardly dare to imagine that such a prospect is open to you. Some are casual about the next step after high school; some are frantic.

Some of you are superior academically, some athletically, some artistically. Some are disciplined, hardworking, and confident; others are confused, falling behind, unable to get through the day much less think about the future.

Even you the individual are in the process of changing from one day to the next. Your body is growing; your mind is in flux. You can feel at the bottom of the heap one moment and on top of the world the next. Outside people and events—a sensitive counselor, an imaginative teacher, an exciting summer experience, a disappointing job, a broken love affair, a parental separation, a family move or illness, a sudden flash of inspiration from a book, a chance discovery of talent for science or art or sport—all these can turn your life upside down.

How can we talk to all of you, all high school students? If you are so diverse a group, is there one language with which we can communicate with all of you?

We cannot reach you all. It would be wonderful if each of you had a personal mentor, a guide at your elbow to show you the best way to deal with the problems and triumphs of teenage life. In place of that ideal guide, we offer this book to enable you to take as much responsibility for your own progress as you possibly can.

Our belief is that, as beginning grown-ups, you can teach yourself the one big skill that will be invaluable to you throughout your life: taking charge. The immediate bonus of taking charge is that high school will be livelier, more interesting, more fulfilling. High school is neither a jail to serve time in until you are let out into the world, nor simply a way station to college.

College is the end result of a long process. Our hope is that this book will stimulate you to tailor that process to your own abilities, talents, and interests. Although each of you is a distinct individual, we have discovered through many years of college advising that there are certain threads of common concern to all of you. Our aim is to address those concerns with clear and concrete suggestions that can be of use to you at any stage in your high school career.

We propose ways to stretch your thinking about yourself and your capabilities. We help you chart your academic program to include rewarding electives as well as the necessary basics. We give you tips on how to avoid boredom in class. We introduce you to techniques that expand your reading, writing, speaking, and study skills. We show you how to manage your time resourcefully and to deal with that familiar bugaboo: procrastination. We highlight methods of troubleshooting academic and personal problems, finding help when you need it, talking to teachers and counselors, and reducing the anxieties of decision making. We steer you to summer resources for earning and learning and advise you on connecting with enjoyable activities that suit your own personality.

The high school years are yours to explore and enjoy. With the help of these guidelines and your own creative effort, you can make getting the most out of high school the ideal countdown to college.

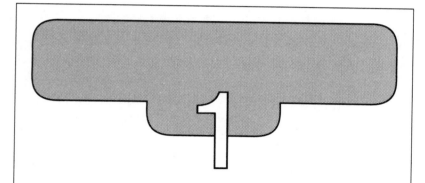

Taking Charge

Ask any group of college students if they're satisfied with what they accomplished in high school and you're likely to hear a lot of "If only I had . . ." statements. Take Karen, for example, who discovered in college that she could have gotten a lot more out of high school—if only she had *really* learned how to study, manage her free time, make good decisions. Or Jim, who could have gotten more out of his four years if only he had tackled interesting internships over the summers; or Sue, if she had participated in some exciting after-school activities. If only they had known then what they know now.

You, who are still in high school, are the lucky ones. You don't have to say "if only. . . ." You are right there now. Even if you haven't had the best beginnings, it is never too late to make the most of your high school years. You are young enough and flexible enough to make changes; you are old enough to take charge of your own life.

Steering Your Way

Taking charge, in fact, may be the most important thing you can learn in high school. If you drift through school, choosing the easy classes, hanging out with friends, not thinking of the future, you are not taking charge. If you let somebody else make decisions for you, you are not taking charge. If you stick with the same crowd when they're not your style anymore, you are not taking charge. And if you assume that you are headed for Ivy U. because your mother went there, or that you're not going to college at all because your father never went, then certainly you are not taking charge.

Taking charge is like learning to drive a car. At first it seems overwhelming. How can you steer and watch the cars on both sides of the road and brake and move into traffic all at the same time? And on top of that, how will you ever learn to parallel park? But you practice and practice because you really want to learn to drive that car and not be dependent on other people to get you where you're going.

Taking charge takes guts. It means trying out new ideas and sometimes making yourself uncomfortable. That is not easy. Taking charge means you won't always know the outcome of your adventure. That can be very scary. Fear is natural and confusion normal. But taking charge means beginning to set goals and make changes, so that you don't end your high school days singing the "if only" blues.

The Big Question

Before you can begin to take charge, you need to go back a step and ask yourself the big question: "Am I getting the most I can out of high school?"

Maybe the answer is "YES!" Maybe you are feeling terrific about yourself. All your courses at school are awesome. You have a fabulous English teacher who understands you and knows what you mean even when you're not sure yourself. Chemistry is clear as crystal. You're working hard, and you're never bored. You have plenty of time for the swim team, debate club, guitar practice, and talking to your friends on the phone. You're class treasurer. You have a good job after school at the video store. You volunteer on Tuesday evenings to read to shut-ins. With all of this you still manage to sleep eight hours a night. You have a great group of friends who don't smoke, drink, or do drugs. You have all the courses you need to apply to the college of your choice, *if* you decide to go to college. And you have begun to think about where the money will come from to pay for it. On the other hand, if you decide *not* to go to college, your family will respect your wishes and not pressure you.

This person is just too good to be true. If you resemble the high school student in this fable, you can throw this book away. Better still, you can tell *us* how you did it!

On Your Mark

Getting the most out of high school doesn't mean that you have to be perfect. It doesn't mean that you have to be the president of the Student Government Association or the star in the spring musical. It doesn't mean that you have to reach all your goals. What it does mean is that you open yourself to new possibilities in your high school and your community.

High school is the place where you can begin to take chances and make mistakes. High school is the place where you can learn that mistakes aren't fatal, and that mistakes can lead to making better decisions the next time.

High school is the place to practice making small decisions, so that when it comes time to make the big ones, you will have more confidence in your judgment.

High school is the place to test some of your untried abilities. Here's where you can discover that venturing into unknown territory is worth the effort.

High school is the place to practice balancing your social life with your studies and your outside interests. There is no better place than high school to take steps toward independence.

The Choice Is Yours

Your high school years will bring about changes in you no matter what you do—changes in your body, your feelings, your mind. There will be days when you feel wiped out and other days when you're bursting with energy. That's the way it goes.

You'll never be able to control everything you do in high school. But that doesn't mean that you have to be content with moving from one class to the next and filling in spare time with whatever happens to come along. It doesn't mean you have to stick with the same friends and the same routine forever. You can make changes—not only in your social and extracurricular life, but also in the classes you take and the way you go about preparing for them. You have more choice than you think you do.

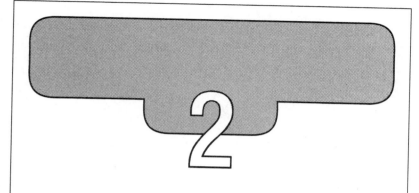

Scheduling a Balanced Academic Program

Andy goes to a suburban school with state-of-the-art facilities; it is known for its high achievers who compete for places in selective colleges.

Wayne goes to an inner-city school with crowded classrooms and outdated lab equipment; most of its students are already working after school, and few aspire to go to college.

Angie is in a magnet school that caters to talented science and math students; 97 percent of its graduates go on to college.

Winona attends a rural school that draws its students from the local farm and factory community; about half plan to enroll at the state university.

This is only a minuscule sample of the students attending the 16,000 diverse public high schools across the country. These schools differ in size, in location, in their course offerings and purpose. There are schools that have 50 students and others that have more than 5,000. They may be urban, suburban, or rural. Some high schools start at ninth grade, some at tenth; others combine junior and senior high. There are academic schools, vocational-technical schools, magnet schools, and alternative schools. In addition to the public schools, there are private and independent (including parochial) schools that are as varied as the public schools.

No matter what school you attend, there's no way to get around it: classes are the center of high school life. Your friends and your social activities are often determined by the classes you take. Your classes affect what you learn and what level of enthusiasm you have for learning. The choices open to you for further study and for college admission depend to a great extent on the courses you take.

Don't Miss Out on the Basics

From a practical point of view, your first step is to make sure that you take all the required subjects. Every school has graduation requirements, and your job is to find out what they are. Most high schools have a process to help you plan your four-year academic schedule so that you don't miss an essential course or a prerequisite for a course. That planning process may include:

- Group orientations or other meetings with high school staff
- Individual conferences with a guidance counselor
- Booklets describing the school's course offerings

What Are the Basics?

No matter what sort of high school you attend—large or small, urban, suburban, or rural—the basic academic subjects for a college preparatory program are the same:

English	4 years
Mathematics	2 years
Science	1 year
Social studies	1 year

Doing your best in these basics will qualify you for entry into your community college or a junior college, as well as a wide choice of state college or state university systems.

Sometimes a basic course in a subject area can propel you into unknown and fascinating territory. When Sally, for example, took the required lab science course, she was introduced to the scientific method by an imaginative teacher who sparked her interest and inspired her to go on to advanced science courses.

Beyond the Basics

Many colleges require a stronger academic program than the basic one listed above. Tackling a tough academic program often provides additional rewards:

- Challenging teachers
- Lively students
- Stimulating discussions
- Small classes

Selective colleges will want to see the following on your transcript:

English	4 years
Foreign language	2 to 4 years
Social studies	2 to 4 years
Mathematics	3 to 4 years
Science	2 to 4 years
The arts	1 year

Quality and Content Count

There are many ways to fulfill the more rigorous requirements listed above. You must make the quality and the content of your courses count.

Four years of *college preparatory* English means getting a thorough background in literature and writing. Some students elect film studies, drama, and journalism in place of traditional English courses. At some schools these electives are rigorous and enriching; at others they may be "gut" courses, easy A's that do not add to your understanding or challenge your abilities.

An elective in the social studies department such as street law or anthropology may be tempting. In some schools, these courses are demanding; in others, they are not.

Since colleges generally cannot judge the quality or the content of such electives, they prefer to see on your record a sequence of traditional English and history courses whose substance is known and clearly defined.

If you are aiming for admission to a selective college, be aware that such a college prefers traditional academic courses over electives of indeterminate content. If you do take courses of questionable substance, arrange for your counselor to write up a description of the courses so that college admissions staff can evaluate them properly.

Finding Outstanding Courses

Your school may have some outstanding courses that don't come under the usual heading of "traditional" — courses that are known for the high quality of subject matter and teaching. Rick, for example, was in a school where the Russian history course was taught by an exceptional teacher who had arranged for his students to be part of an exchange program with the Soviet Union. Bettina's school had an excellent humanities and philosophy course taught by a team of the best teachers; they made the "great books" come alive. In Marcy's high school, an unusual art history program explored the painting and sculpture of the past and also introduced students to contemporary artists.

Courses in your school with a well-deserved reputation for excellence are worth considering when you are making out your schedule. Just be sure you have included the basics and left room for advanced courses you may want to take in traditional subjects.

Making Decisions about Advanced Courses

If you are headed in the direction of the most selective colleges, the ones that encourage rigorous academic preparation, you may want to take the highest-level courses your school offers (see chapter 7).

On the other hand, you may wonder if you should take an advanced math, physics, or language course if you don't have a strong interest in the topic. You may also be concerned that

16

you will get a mediocre grade in a tough course. There isn't one answer to this dilemma.

Let's look at each academic area on its own.

Higher Functions?

For some students, math is a natural. Calculus has always figured in their calculations. But what if math doesn't come easily to you? Should you go on beyond the basic requirements?

There is no question that any student hoping for college admission *must* get through the gateway of algebra. But many students ask, "Do I need to go beyond the algebra sequence into higher math functions?" Again, there isn't one simple answer for everyone.

If you are doing poorly in math and you are struggling with other subjects, you may want to postpone higher math until you get to college.

But some students stop automatically because they tremble at the very thought of fractions or parallelograms. They are anxious about numbers in any shape or form and tend to avoid higher math. It is wise to recognize the anxiety but unwise to avoid the subject. Sometimes removing the fear can spark an unsuspected interest. (See For Your Information at the end of this chapter for a helpful book on math anxiety.)

If at this point you aren't sure of your future goals, and if you are generally a good student who can handle academic challenges, don't rule out going as far as you can in the math sequence in high school. It can make a difference in later options for college or career.

You may ask, "What's wrong with waiting until I get to college to take advanced math?"

A good reason not to wait is that once you get away from math, it's harder to pick it up again. In addition, as one calculus teacher told us, "It's better to take that math course in high school. Introductory calculus is better taught in high school than in college. College math classes are huge, and there is little chance to ask questions. The person who's not a talented math student can easily get lost."

Scientific Connections

As much as high schools differ, most expect students to take an introductory biology course. Students generally don't go on to advanced biology or chemistry unless it is of special interest.

But what about physics?

If you're thinking of building bridges or digging canals or designing skyscrapers, physics is a necessity in high school. You cannot do without high school physics if you are contemplating a career in engineering or architecture.

But suppose these specializations are not in your plans— should you take physics?

One high school math and science teacher gives physics the highest priority for the general student as well as the scientifically talented. "No thinking adult," he says, "can afford to be ignorant of the workings of the world. Physics extends into all areas of living. More and more people are recognizing the connection between physics and philosophy, physics and cosmology. And even religious thinkers are looking more closely at the physical beginnings of the universe."

Don't stay away from physics simply because you're not thinking of a career in science.

Parlez-Vous, Sprechen Sie, Habla Usted?

Study of a foreign language is increasingly becoming a requirement for entry into college. But what about going on beyond the basic requirement? You've taken two years of Spanish, let's say. Should you drop language altogether? Should you try another language?

If the teaching is good and you're gaining more and more competency, you should go as far as you can in the language you've already begun. You will be amazed at the pleasure you find when you pass the elementary plateau and begin speaking with some fluency and reading the literature of the country.

Colleges in general report that they prefer that students persist in a language rather than jump from one to another or drop language entirely. In addition, many colleges require proficiency in one foreign language as part of their own graduation requirements. If you've already gained that proficiency in high school, your foreign-language options in college are more flexible. You may choose to test out of the college requirement; you may decide to go on to more advanced courses in your language; or you may want to begin a new language.

Equally important, facility in a foreign language will open opportunities for travel and contact with another people and another culture. And many programs—for summers and college junior year abroad—are open only to those with proficiency in a foreign language.

Why Bother with a Heavy Schedule?

Why load yourself down with a heavy schedule of courses that take extra work when you can get by with a lot less?

Apart from providing the satisfying rewards that usually accompany these courses, you will be preparing yourself for college-level work.

To Andy college seemed a long way off. His complaint was that his classes were boring and took too much time away from soccer, drums, and friends. He hadn't yet recognized the advantages, both present and future, of a strong academic program.

"College," said Karen, "is a lot harder than high school. My friends who had a really strong high school program were so much better prepared than I was. They didn't have to waste time making up in college what they missed in high school. They could choose the more exciting college courses."

Scheduling Your Program

With help from the guidance staff, plan your academic program to make sure you schedule all the requirements.

If your interests are in English and history, you may want to forgo some of the more advanced math or science courses; similarly, if you're a math or science whiz, you may choose more of those subjects in place of history and English electives.

```
TIPS ON SORTING OUT CURRICULUM

• What is special about your school's curriculum?

• How far does the math sequence go?

• What choice do you have in science courses?

• Are there some outstanding, nontraditional courses?

• Are there language courses such as Latin, Russian, Japanese,
  or Chinese?

• Do certain departments have exceptional teachers?
```

Overall, you should aim for a well-balanced program that includes as rigorous a course of study as you can handle without neglecting the especially worthwhile electives. You may not want, nor is it desirable, to take a full load of heavy academic courses every semester. Francine, for example, continually filled her schedule with tough academic courses and became so burdened with homework and papers that she didn't have time for anything else. She couldn't explore art, music, photography, woodworking, or any other possible interests.

The key to a good schedule is balancing requirements and interests. There is no one formula that suits everybody.

For Your Information

Boyer, Ernest L. *High School: A Report on Secondary Education in America*. The Carnegie Foundation for the Advancement of Teaching. New York: Harper and Row, 1983.

Casserly, Patricia Lund. *Helping Able Young Women Take Math and Science Seriously in School*. New York: College Entrance Examination Board, 1979.

The College Board. *Academic Preparation for College: What Students Need to Know and Be Able to Do*. New York: College Entrance Examination Board, 1983.

Groening, Matt. *School Is Hell*. New York: Pantheon, 1987.

Tobias, Sheila. *Succeed with Math: Every Student's Guide to Conquering Math Anxiety*. New York: College Entrance Examination Board, 1987.

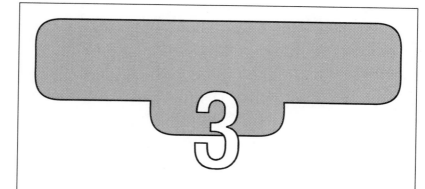

Tackling the Big Skills: Reading, Writing, Speaking

"The ability to handle language, to integrate language, and to apply language is the most important goal of learning," says Ernest L. Boyer, president of the Carnegie Foundation for the Advancement of Teaching. These skills—reading, writing, and speaking—are the essential tools of communication. High school is the ideal time and place to sharpen them.

Discovering Books

Talking about what had helped him most in his career, a foreign service officer who had risen to the rank of ambassador said, "Reading. There's no question about it. My father was a salesman, and we didn't have much money. The public library was free. That meant the whole world was open to me, just as it was to boys whose fathers were doctors and lawyers and businessmen. If it weren't for the library, I would never have had a scholarship to college, I would never have passed the foreign service exam, I would never have been able to compete with others from a more privileged background."

Some people are lucky. Their houses are filled with books. Their parents read to them from the time they are babies. They grow up with books as part of their everyday life. But that is unusual. Most of the time young people have to discover books on their own.

Discovering books is different from reading an assignment in a textbook. The textbook is just that: assigned. You have no choice. When you read a textbook, you read for the information in it; you read because it will be on a test; you read because someone has told you to.

Even in an English class, the reading is, for the most part, not of your own choosing. You may groan over *Hamlet*; *The Scarlet Letter* may not be your cup of tea. But books, and the ideas in them, are as wide as the world, and as exciting, once you get started.

The Rewards of Reading

People who develop a love of reading have a special advantage in life. They don't ever need to be bored, even when they're alone. They can talk with other people who read. They can develop interesting friends because they themselves are interesting. They can help themselves overcome poverty, difficult home situations, even poor schooling.

From a practical point of view, the rewards of reading cannot be emphasized enough. It is through reading that you gradually collect a store of information, as well as a sense of how to express ideas, and the vocabulary to do it.

There is no cram course in comprehension or vocabulary that can substitute for consistent reading. Often before taking the SATs or other college admissions tests students frantically try to shove into their heads a technique for absorbing and understanding paragraphs, along with five years' worth of word definitions. One high school junior started copying words from the dictionary on yellow stickums and pasting them up all over the house. She never got beyond the A's and B's, and she forgot most of those definitions an hour after she learned them. Cramming can't take the place of making words a part of your life through regular reading.

TV and Movies Aren't the Answer

You can learn a great deal from TV and movies, but they are not substitutes for books. TV and movies are in some ways more limiting. You see the action through the eyes of the people who have made the show. The director chooses the shots for you. The camera is there, depicting the scene for you. The casting director has chosen the actors. Choose a different actor, and you have a different portrait. Decorate the background in a different way, and you have a different emphasis.

This is especially evident when you see a novel translated to the screen. Ellen had read *Heidi* over and over again as a child. When she saw it on the screen, she was furious. "That," she said, "is not *my* Heidi. That's not what she looks like, not how she talks. The Grandfather is all wrong. And the mountain cabin, and the field, and the goatherd, Peter. All wrong. Even the cheese they eat is the wrong shape."

Juanita said that when she read the spooky novel *Dracula* she was so terrified that for days she couldn't sleep. Some time later she saw the movie version. "I laughed," she said. "I wasn't scared at all. What was in my head was so much more real, and so much more interesting."

You don't need to scare yourself to death to realize that reading a book can be a more vivid experience than having it all dressed up and set out for you on the screen. When you read, it is just between you and the writer. The writer is your companion. True, you can't argue with the writer, or ask a question in person. But on the other hand, you can turn away without insulting the author; you can put the book down and take it up again at any time. You can skip parts that don't interest you, or that you want to save for later. You can read the same paragraph over and over again if it isn't clear the first time. You can carry a book with you and read it at any time—on the bus, in the doctor's office, while you wait for a friend who forgot what time it was.

Open Bookshelves

One of the greatest advantages of being a book reader is that you are your own boss. You have an endless choice of subjects, writers, periods, countries. Until you explore the world of books, you have no idea how much variety there is. In *Good Books*, Steven Gilbar provides a list of books categorized according to subject. The subjects range from A to Z, with ballet, baseball, computers, divorce, jazz, loneliness, rock and roll, and Vietnam war in between. Thousands of books on hundreds of subjects.

If you're not in the habit of picking up a book, you can

start in a number of ways. One way *is* by subject matter. Start with something that interests you. Look into a compendium like *Good Books* for suggestions.

Browsing

Browsing in the library also affords an excellent opportunity to get started on your reading habit. Every public library, no matter how small or large, has the same system for shelving books. A section for fiction, a section for biography, and numbered sections for nonfiction subjects, like religion, history, law, gardening, cooking, travel. Browse and discover those sections in which you feel most at home.

Browse also among the magazines. The library usually will allow you to check out all but the most current issues of magazines. Again, the subject matter is wide-ranging: from mechanics and cars to baseball and tennis; from fashion to politics; from science to literary essays. Articles instead of books, short stories instead of novels—these are ways of establishing the reading habit.

You might browse in the young people's section. Books you read as a child, books you wish you had read as a child, are all there for you. Some of the most talented writers have written for children. One high school senior had never read *Winnie the Pooh* until he was babysitting for a neighbor. "What great, funny stories those are! I wish somebody had read them to me when I was a kid, but they make me laugh just as much now. I know I'll read them to my kids."

Books for teenagers—fiction as well as nonfiction dealing with all sorts of subjects, including the problems high school students face—are also shelved in the young people's section. Librarians in this section are especially trained to help students.

Book Reviews

It's a good idea to become familiar with the book reviews in the daily and Sunday newspapers and in the news magazines.

They deal with books on all sorts of subjects. Reviews of the same book by different people can prove to you that not everybody has the same taste and can give you the courage to judge for yourself what is useful or pointless, interesting or dull.

Finding Time for Reading

We hear students complain, "But I don't have time to read on my own. I have to keep up with my homework and help around the house, go to practice. There's no time left."

With a crowded schedule, finding time to read is a problem. You may have to look over your daily schedule (see chapter 4) to find a way to steal time from other activities to establish the reading habit. You may discover, for instance, that you are watching TV for more hours than you think or spending much more than "just five minutes" on the telephone. Once you make

---

READING TIPS

- Carry a book on the bus, to a doctor's office—any place you may have expected or unexpected spare moments.
- Ask a good friend to read the same book you're reading. Talk about it later.
- Jot down ideas from books that you agree or disagree with.
- As you read, jot down new words in a small notebook. Look them up later. Use one or two new words a week in your conversation.
- Ask the librarian for books in your field of interest.
- Ask your friends or older sister or brother to recommend books.
- Clip reviews of books you might like to read and put them in a folder.
- Ask for a special book or magazine subscription as a birthday present.
- Make reading a habit.

---

reading a priority, you will be surprised at the amount of time you can find for it.

Putting Ideas into Words

To get your ideas across to other people, to convince people of your point of view, you need to be able to write clearly and forcefully. Writing skills are essential for

- Getting into college
- Succeeding in college
- Landing a job
- Advancing in that job

But many high school students do not know how to write well. One high school English teacher says, "Even some of my best students don't know how to write. I'm not talking about their punctuation, grammar, and spelling—I'm talking about organizing ideas in a logical way so that other people can understand what they're trying to say."

Many students simply haven't practiced enough to develop good writing skills. Often schools ask students to fill in the blanks instead of writing answers in full sentences.

Some teachers have tried to bridge the gap. "I do a lot with essay questions in my classes," said one history teacher. "I think writing should be practiced across the board—in history, biology, as well as English. But teachers are pressed for time, and many of them can't put out the extra effort it takes to read and grade essays."

That's true. So if writing is not a high priority in your school, you have to do as much as possible on your own. Your teachers can help you, and there are books listed at the end of this chapter that can give you guidance. But the most important advice for learning any skill can be summed up in one simple word: *practice*.

Practice Writing

There are many ways to practice writing. Buy yourself a new notebook and use it as a journal, writing down your thoughts, hopes, opinions. Not only is it good practice, but you will get a real kick out of looking back, next year or in 10 years, at the person you once were.

Write out in sentences everything you can: notes on assignments, things to do, messages to friends. If you keep at it, writing won't seem so strange to you. Writing will become more natural and not so much of a chore when it's time to hand in an essay.

When your teachers give you the option of a diorama or poster or written report, choose the report. In the beginning you may find it more difficult, but as you practice organizing the material and shaping it in your own way, you will gain in competency. Your reward: satisfaction.

Write letters. Write to your grandmother. Try to make your letters as interesting as you can. You know what it feels like to find a long newsy letter in the mailbox. Write letters and you'll get letters back.

Not only is writing an essential tool; it can be an exciting way to discover the feelings and thoughts you didn't know you had. One writer of short stories says, "I never know how the

---

WRITING TIPS

- Put down the phone, pick up your pen.
- Choose one or two writers you like and try imitating their style.
- Correspond with a student in another city or another country.
- Write a story for a younger sister, brother, or neighbor.
- Write a poem for a friend's birthday.
- When studying a book for a test, read a section and then write it out in your own words.

---

characters are going to act until I start putting them down on paper. They always surprise me."

Expressing your feelings and thoughts in your journal, in a letter, or in a story can teach you a lot about yourself.

Writing out a personal problem instead of mulling it over in your head can sometimes help you find a solution.

Reading and writing go together. When you read good books, you absorb ideas, technique, and style that improve your own writing. When you write, you clarify and develop your ideas. Whether you are writing fact or fiction, you explore your ideas to express the best of yourself to others.

Speak Out

The importance of speaking out, speaking clearly, speaking intelligently is another skill that cannot be emphasized enough. In a sense, you are on stage all your life. Your own self-confidence, as well as the effect you have on other people, depends on what you say and how you say it. You may look handsome or beautiful, but the world quickly gets past that first impression. You may be brilliant, but it will be impossible for anyone to guess what innovative thoughts are in your head unless you speak out.

Speak Up

There's no better place to start your speaking career than in high school. Here, you are surrounded by people your own age, most of them just as self-conscious as you. Almost everyone is shy about speaking up in class.

"I'm afraid I'll be boring."

"What if somebody laughs?"

"Who wants to be a blabbermouth?"

"I hate those people who are always sticking up their hands and answering questions. Why would I want to be like that?"

All this is a cop-out. Sure it's a risk to speak up. But remember, you're not exactly facing a firing squad—just a bunch of high school kids like yourself, most of whom will admire you for having courage. There are many reasons to take the risk:

- Making the decision to speak will help you with your studying by forcing you to prepare and organize before you reach the classroom.

- Unless you are reacting, responding, questioning, you are not really learning. When you listen passively, your mind wanders. You are not involved. Later, you will find it much harder to remember the material and to make intelligent use of it. When you speak up, you will remember what you said about the subject under discussion.

- Through speaking out, you will gradually learn that you have as much to say, and can say it as well, as anybody else. Being "on stage" in the classroom will increase your confidence in all areas.

- Your teachers will be grateful for the feedback. They need to have students respond to their ideas. And, as your teachers get to know you, they will be far better able to write whatever recommendations are needed when you apply for jobs or college.

- Speaking up in class prepares you for important interviews. Whether you are being interviewed for a summer job, an internship, or a college admission, how you express yourself is vitally important. The interviewer is not your best friend who knows what is in your heart and mind. He or she listens to you only for a brief time. You need practice making the most of those minutes.

Ask the Right Questions

A good way for you to get started speaking up is to practice asking questions. There is no such thing as a stupid question if you are well prepared and if you have listened attentively to what went on before. Remember, if something is not clear to you, you can be sure that many other students are in the same fix. They will thank you for asking for an explanation.

Think about your best teachers. How do they get across ideas and concepts? Are they good teachers because of their ability to speak about the material clearly?

Teachers welcome good questions. Sometimes a teacher doesn't know that a point has not been emphasized strongly enough. Generally, a teacher is pleased to be questioned and pleased to clarify, providing that the question shows the student has been listening and absorbing.

Asking questions, or speaking up on a subject, doesn't mean monopolizing the classroom discussion. Don't worry that you'll get a reputation as a general nuisance. The right question at the right time can only bring respect from those who needed to know but didn't dare to ask.

But how do you come up with good questions or comments and feel comfortable voicing them? The chart on Speaking Tips provides some suggestions.

SPEAKING TIPS

- As you do your homework, think of what needs further explanation. Prepare a question. Write it down.
- If you disagree with another student, say so and be prepared to back it up.
- Start speaking and questioning in the class in which you feel most at ease with the subject, most comfortable with the teacher.
- Develop your confidence by joining the debate team, the forensics society, or the drama club.

Be honest with yourself in evaluating your performance as a speaker. Ask the following questions:

- Is my voice clear and confident?
- Do I express myself without too many hesitations and "you-knows"?
- Do I have the correct words to express what I want to say?
- Do I develop a thought in a clear and interesting way?

Such constructive criticism will ultimately serve to bolster both your performance and your confidence as a speaker.

For Your Information

Gilbar, Steven. *Good Books: A Book Lover's Companion*. New York: Ticknor and Fields, 1982.

Koch, Kenneth. *Wishes, Lies, and Dreams: Teaching Children to Write Poetry*. New York: Harper and Row, 1980.

Koch, Kenneth, and Kate Farrell. *Sleeping on the Wing: An Anthology of Modern Poetry with Essays on Reading and Writing*. New York: Random House, 1981.

Stillman, Peter. *Writing Your Way*. Upper Montclair, N.J.: Boynton/ Cook Publishers, 1984.

Strunk, William, Jr., and E. B. White. *The Elements of Style*. 3d ed. New York: Macmillan, 1979.

Tchudi, Susan, and Stephen Tchudi. *The Young Writer's Handbook*. New York: Scribner's, 1984.

Van Doren, Charles. *The Joy of Reading*. New York: Harmony Books, 1985.

Zinsser, William. *On Writing Well*. 3d ed. New York: Harper and Row, 1988.

Zinsser, William. *Writing to Learn*. New York: Harper and Row, 1988.

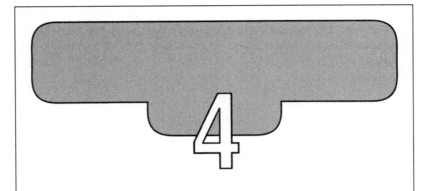

Organizing
Time and Space

J aime Escalante, the math teacher on whose life the movie *Stand and Deliver* is based, said it this way: "The teacher is just the coach. Students can't just sit on the bench; they have to play the game."

A guidance counselor in a large suburban high school said it another way: "I see a lot of students who are unprepared for class, late with assignments, and generally disorganized. Halfway through high school they get panicky and want to do something about it. I can help them, but the responsibility for doing the right thing is on their shoulders."

"Playing the game" and "doing the right thing" are different ways of saying "taking charge." Most of you probably think that your power to control your destiny in high school is quite limited. You are told what courses to take, when an assignment is due, what pages to read in the text for Thursday, what will be on a test, and what conjugations to memorize. There doesn't seem to be much of a chance to make choices.

But there is room within the system for you to "play the game." As discussed in chapters 2 and 3, you can set up the academic program that will give you the best that your high school offers, and you can set goals for yourself to gain solid communication skills. In addition, you can learn to control your own time and organize your life to better enjoy what you're doing. Mastering such skills will help you get the most out of high school.

What Time Is It?

Elana, a college student, told us that one of the essentials she learned in high school was handling her time. "I had to make up my mind to organize my schedule and stick to it. I worked very hard at it and found there really was enough time for study *and* play."

The time-management skills that you learn and practice in high school will come in handy for anything you attempt later on in your life. "All of us have the same amount of time," says a college dean of students. "How we utilize it is what can make a difference."

Time Wasters

There are several big time wasters that students have to look out for:

- An inability to say "no"
- Excessive socializing on the telephone
- Random TV watching
- Fatigue
- Underestimating the time it takes to do a task
- Attempting to do too much

The examples of five students show how big blocks of time can be used up by various activities:

- Julie can't say "no" when her friends call on the phone for long social chats.
- Raoul flips the dial and lets the TV set steal two or three hours out of his day.
- Brian shoots baskets for hours every afternoon and then feels he needs a long nap.
- Laurie's after-school time is totally taken up with student government, cheerleading, dancing lessons, and a part-time job.
- Amy puts off all her assignments to the last minute and then uses up valuable hours worrying about what she's not doing.

Most students would be surprised to know where the time has gone. Julie and her friends agreed to take the advice of their counselor and to make exact note of where their time went every day for a week. See the chart Julie's Typical Day to find out how Julie spent her time.

JULIE'S TYPICAL DAY

Start	End	Time Used	Activity/Description
6:00	6:01	1 min	Alarm goes off, wake up
6:01	6:21	20 min	Shower
6:21	6:36	15 min	Dress
6:36	6:42	6 min	Eat breakfast
6:42	6:54	12 min	Brush teeth, straighten up room, pack up school bag
6:54	7:03	9 min	Make lunch
7:03	7:30	27 min	Leave for bus, arrive at school
7:30	8:00	30 min	Go to locker, talk with friends
8:00	2:30	6 hrs, 30 min	School
2:30	3:00	30 min	Bus home
3:00	4:00	1 hr	TV and snack
4:00	4:20	20 min	Practice piano
4:20	5:00	40 min	Talk on phone
5:00	6:30	1 hr, 30 min	Listen to radio, watch TV, mess around: comb hair, clean up room, dance, play with dog
6:30	7:00	30 min	Set table, talk to mom
7:00	7:30	30 min	Dinner
7:30	8:00	30 min	Practice piano, talk on phone
8:00	8:30	30 min	Watch TV, talk on phone
8:30	9:00	30 min	Talk on phone
9:00	9:45	45 min	Homework
9:45	10:00	15 min	Get ready for bed, read a while, sleep

Julie saw after looking at her typical day that she was leaving her homework until late in the evening, and that she was spending much more time than she had imagined talking to friends on the phone. Her parents' nagging about phone calls had not had any effect, but now she realized she had to make some changes.

Taking Account of Your Time

You can use a similar chart to keep an exact record of each day for a week. Jot down everything you do from the moment you wake up until you turn out your light. Of course, put in your scheduled classes and your commitments like soccer practice, clubs, piano lessons, and job. Note how much time you spend eating breakfast, getting to school, chatting with friends. Don't leave anything out. Don't change your schedule to fit an ideal of what you think you ought to be doing. Don't make any judgments; just observe yourself.

YOUR TYPICAL DAY

Start	End	Time Used	Activity/Description

After filling out the schedule, you will have a better idea of how you are spending your time. Maybe you tend to set aside hours for specific tasks and then find that distractions have taken over. Or maybe you are devoting too much time to kicking the soccer ball around, listening to music, or talking to friends. Maybe you think too much about what you should be doing instead of doing it.

Answer the questions in the chart Do You Know Where Your Time Goes? (next page) to get a better idea about how you are spending your time.

Time for a Change

Once you know how you spend your typical day and where your time goes, you may recognize that it's time for a change. If you find you don't have enough hours for homework and study, perhaps you need to set your own specific limits on telephoning, TV watching, and socializing on school nights. If you're overly involved in after-school activities, perhaps you can give up a club or shorten your hours on the job. Make your time work for you by beginning to modify your routine.

Here is how the five students mentioned earlier in this chapter decided to make changes:

- Julie told her friends that on school nights she would receive calls only between 7:30 and 8:00.
- Raoul looked over the TV schedule at the beginning of each week, made a conscious choice of what programs he would watch, and limited himself to those.
- Brian decided to play basketball an hour a day and found he didn't need an afternoon nap.
- Laurie realized why her grades were plummeting and decided that she would have to eliminate at least one of her after-school activities.
- Amy determined to keep to her schedule for doing assignments to avoid wasting time on deadline anxiety.

Do You Know Where Your Time Goes?

Do you usually know in the morning how you will spend your
day after class? Yes _____ No _____

Does each school day include enough time

for study? Yes _____ No _____

for hobbies and sports? Yes _____ No _____

for friends? Yes _____ No _____

for chores? Yes _____ No _____

for sleep? Yes _____ No _____

Do you put limits on

watching TV? Yes _____ No _____

talking on the telephone? Yes _____ No _____

listening to music? Yes _____ No _____

taking naps? Yes _____ No _____

messing around? Yes _____ No _____

Do you hand in your assignments on time?

Yes _____ No _____

Do you know how much time to set aside for each assignment?

Yes _____ No _____

Do you do hard tasks first and save the easy ones for later?

Yes _____ No _____

Do you know how to turn down distracting invitations?

Yes _____ No _____

TIPS FOR SAVING TIME

- Prepare your clothes the night before so you'll have time for a good breakfast.
- Get up 15 minutes earlier in order to review your notes, read the morning paper, or think about the day's classes.
- Use those odd spare minutes that are now in the lost column to write an overdue letter, work on a math problem, clean out your desk, or look up a word in the dictionary.
- Try doing two things at once if they don't require full concentration. While watching TV, for instance, you might reorganize your notebook or do aerobic exercises.
- Recite French verb conjugations or history dates while you're biking, jogging, or swimming laps.
- Bring a book to read or study while you wait for a dentist or doctor appointment.

Sometimes you can find five or more hours a week by revising the way you've been doing things. By creatively using small blocks of time, by doing certain tasks together, you can stretch the day.

Possibly you can make better use of your time if you discover periods of the day when you work more efficiently. When you are filling out your time chart, you might make note of those hours when you feel most energetic and use those times for your hardest tasks.

By observing how you spend your time and creating a schedule that is good for you, you can lead a more rewarding life. You may have to experiment to get the right balance of work and play, but remember, time is yours to use as *you* think best.

Are You a Procrastinator?

Almost everyone puts off doing some important tasks for another time, but there are those who constantly postpone their assignments, thinking that there will be plenty of time to do them later.

Larry, for example, watches TV until 10 o'clock at night, at which point he is much too tired to work on his math problems or read his history text.

Jean reads her novel for three hours after dinner and then has no time to do a good job on her English composition. She keeps asking for extensions when her papers are due.

Bryce tinkers with his bicycle, reviews baseball scores with his brother, talks to his girlfriend on the phone, and then finds the evening has slipped away before he can look over his chemistry formulas for tomorrow's quiz.

These three students live constantly under a cloud of heavy tension. They know they're running late most of the time, but they feel they're unable to do anything about it. "I know I procrastinate," says Bryce, "but I can't help myself."

If you are a procrastinator, you'll find yourself answering "yes" to the following questions:

- Do you do nonessentials first and put off the vital tasks until later?
- Do you get absorbed in a magazine and then not have enough time to finish homework?
- Do you usually hand in your assignments late?
- Are you often anxious because you're rushing to meet deadlines?
- Do you spend a lot of time figuring out excuses for handing in an assignment after the deadline has passed?
- Do you think things have gotten out of control?

One expert who has looked into such patterns of procrastination found that the habitual "latecomer" usually starts the day saying, "I'm late, I'm late." A high school boy, for example, oversleeps because he's spent the previous night trying to catch up on yesterday's assignments. He rushes through the morning routine, wasting precious minutes deciding what to wear to school, and then has no time to eat breakfast. He's late for the bus anyway and late for the first class. Harried and tense, often unprepared, he loses interest in what's going on in his courses. When he gets home from school, he fools around with all the nonessentials and then has no time to do the things that *have* to be done.

In addition, the procrastinator plays "chicken" with deadlines by giving himself one excuse after another. It's as if he were driving a car when the gas gauge is on "empty" and assuming that those last few drops will be enough to get him where he wants to go, or that a gas station will turn up at the magic moment. This kind of driving makes for severe anxiety.

And so the procrastinator wastes time on disorganization and worry. The quality of work he or she does manage to finish is never as high as it might be. Grades suffer; confidence is undermined.

Why Do You Procrastinate?

You may well ask, "How did things get this way?"

Psychologists say that procrastination sometimes starts out as a way of saying "no" to parents or teachers. The trouble is that when you start out saying "no" to others, you can wind up saying "no" to yourself, and getting in the way of what you really want to accomplish.

Larry, for instance, didn't want *anyone* to tell him when to do his homework, yet he couldn't get himself to do it even though he wanted to pull up his grades.

Procrastination can also be an excuse for not doing top-quality work. Jean, for example, thought of herself as a creative writer, but by not having enough time to do a first-rate job on her compositions, she always had an excuse for not measuring up to her own expectations.

Procrastination can also be a way of dealing with unrealistic goals. Bryce wanted to excel in the same tough honors courses that his older brother had sailed through with all A's. When he couldn't match his brother's record, Bryce began to avoid the work and let time slide by instead of realistically looking for help or readjusting his schedule.

Stopping the Habit

If you have developed a habit of delaying, dallying, putting off, you can also stop the habit. But like the overeater or the smoker, you have to exert effort and develop patience in order to bring about change. One or two successes, as good as they feel, are not enough to break the habit.

Follow the Tips for the Procrastinator in the accompanying chart, and you'll be pleased with the results.

Start by taking control. Even the fellow who drives his car on "empty" all the time *can* learn to fill his tank when the gauge reads a quarter full!

TIPS FOR THE PROCRASTINATOR

- Set up a list of priorities *each* day.
- Put assignments that have a deadline on the top of your list.
- Put nonessentials at the bottom of your list.
- Force yourself to follow the list in order.
- Check off each item as you complete it. Checking items off gives you a visible sign of your accomplishments and makes you feel good.
- Divide long-term assignments into bits and pieces.
- Compel yourself to do a bit or a piece each day, no matter how hard.
- Set shorter deadlines for yourself. Instead of playing "chicken," play "beat the clock."
- Reward yourself after each finished task.

Easing Parental Pressure

Organizing time and breaking the procrastination habit can be a big help when it comes to parental pressure. Parents get anxious when they think you are neglecting your schoolwork and wasting time. Many students report that their parents are constantly nagging them: stop talking on the phone, stop watching TV, stop playing video games.

How can you put their fears to rest? One way is to show them that you have a plan and that it includes getting your work done. You might consider making a simple agreement with them:

- No matter how much I may be fussing around, I will have breakfast before I go to school.
- Even though I may sometimes be watching TV or speaking to friends on the phone, I have set my own limits and will get my homework done before I go to bed.
- If I don't live up to my end of the bargain, you have the right to talk to me about it.

If you stick to a realistic agreement, you will be surprised at how the pressure and the arguments will fade away.

Where Did You Put It? Organizing Your Work Area

When Debby looked over her time schedule, she discovered how many hours she wasted looking for her keys, her socks, her assignment book. Realizing that she couldn't afford to lose all that time, she resolved to simplify her life by having a place for everything. One of her first tasks was to choose one specific place to keep all her books and papers and to do her schoolwork.

No matter how small the space you work in, make it your own. Arrange your materials so that you can put your hands on what you want when you need it. Basic needs include:

- A table or desk
- A good reading light
- A box with pens and pencils
- A supply of looseleaf notebook paper

Debby thought she might visit an office supply shop to look for things to get her life in order. She was surprised to find a large variety of articles that gave her new ideas on how she could regroup.

Office supply stores provide many additional items to help you establish an efficient home setup. Beyond the basics, you will find:

- File boxes
- Date books
- Paper clips
- Bulletin boards
- Folders
- Memo pads

You might want to walk through your nearest office supply store and see if you can spot things that suit your particular needs.

Although you've established your special place, there may be times when you will work temporarily elsewhere. If you do occasionally work on your bed or at the kitchen table, make sure you return everything to your regular work space. Even if you do your studying at the library, you still need a specific place in the house for your books and papers.

Organizing Your Notebook and Assignments

The high school student's main piece of equipment is a good notebook. The most useful kind is a sturdy looseleaf book with a hard cover. On the first day of the new term, you'll need to arrange your notebook with dividers, preferably color-coded so that you can easily identify each subject. Keep a good supply of looseleaf paper and reinforcements in your locker as well as at home, and make a habit of cleaning out your notebook regularly.

If you keep assignments on scraps of paper, they will likely get into the washing machine along with your jeans. Instead, you should develop a method and a routine for knowing what your assignments are and what you'll need in order to do them. One way to keep assignments in order is to clip a small book to your notebook. Be sure to check your assignment book before leaving school so that you can take home whatever materials you need to do your homework.

It goes without saying that your notebook, assignment book, and other school gear should be carried in a book bag, tote bag, or knapsack. Carrying such gear in your arms is not only cumbersome but risky: you may inadvertently lose an important item.

Lifetime Skills

Organizing your space and managing your time will help you gain control, making an enormous difference in what you accomplish in high school and in how you feel about yourself. These are skills for now and for the rest of your life.

For Your Information

Colligen, Louise, and Doug Colligen. *Scholastic's A-Plus Guide to Good Grades*. New York: Scholastic, 1979.
Eisenberg, Ronni, and Kate Kelly. *Organizing Yourself*. New York: Macmillan, 1986.
Winston, Stephanie. *Getting Organized*. New York: Warner Books, 1978.

What Do You Hear? What Do You Know? Listening, Taking Notes, Studying

Everybody knows someone in school who gets terrific grades, knows all the answers in class, but doesn't seem to spend much time studying. Most students think that this person is a "genius" and that genius comes strictly from genes. Or maybe they think the "genius" has learned some magic secrets for studying.

But in fact, you don't have to be a genius, and there is no magic, and there are no secrets for good study skills. Listening, note taking, and studying are not skills you are born with; they are skills you can learn.

What Is Listening?

Sam gets to class, puts his books on his desk, and then fastens his eyes on his English teacher. He knows the subject is Shakespeare, and he catches a few words like "Macbeth" and "witches." In reality, his thoughts are on whether to ask Judy or Maria to the basketball game on Friday. Although he thinks he is listening, he ends up without a clue as to what his English teacher has said. He figures he can catch up with the subject later when he studies the textbook.

Listening is different from hearing. Hearing is strictly mechanical. With good ears, anyone can hear. Listening has to be learned. You have to practice, just the way you would practice the piano or hoop shots. Paying attention to words and sentences is the first key to understanding facts and ideas.

Applying the technique of listening in the classroom gives you the following scholastic advantages:

- Your classes will be more interesting.
- You will be alert.
- You will take better notes.
- You will pinpoint essential study themes.
- You will use your study time more efficiently.

- Your grades will certainly improve.
- You will banish boredom.

But how do you know if you are listening or just hearing?

> Do you say the subject is dull?
> Do you think your teachers are boring?
> Do you get distracted by every sound in the classroom?
> Do you sit as far back in the room as possible?
> Do you daydream in class much of the time?
> Do you give up listening when the subject gets complicated?
> Do you decide not to listen because you can read it all in the textbook?

Answering "yes" to most of these questions probably just confirms what you already know: that things are going in one ear and out the other. Although these questions may seem very different, "yes" answers all amount to the same thing: you have opted out of listening.

Let's take a closer look at these questions.

The Problem of Boredom

You think the subject is dull and the teacher boring. Well, it is true that not every subject or every teacher is entertaining. There are some teachers who can make any subject lively, and when you get them you're in for a treat. But treats are special; struggling with boredom in the classroom is a more common problem. Even if you could switch subjects and teachers at will, you wouldn't always solve the boredom problem. But if you let boredom take over, it can spoil your entire high school experience.

So what can you do about boredom? You can change your approach.

Cures for Boredom

The best cure is to *take action*. If you actively participate instead of sitting in a permanent state of numbness, you are bound to improve the quality of your classroom experience. A change in your point of view will help you approach your studies in a more positive way.

You need to make things different. Fire up your imagination. You have plenty of imagination when it comes to daydreaming, passing notes, mimicking the teacher. Now come up with some ways to make the boring class more interesting to you.

Joe got an idea for making his history class less boring when he attended the school production of *Romeo and Juliet*. There weren't any seats in the back, where he usually sat. He took a seat in the first row and discovered that sitting up close made a big difference. He noticed the way the actors looked and moved, and he heard words he didn't know were in the play. He decided to experiment with sitting in the first row in his history class to get himself more involved in the classroom action.

Nicole was falling asleep during a grammar review in her English class. She felt she knew most of what the teacher was saying, and she was tired of hearing it. One day, out of desperation, she began to think of all the ways the rules didn't work. Whenever the teacher cited a rule of grammar, Nicole tried to think of an exception. Finding exceptions to the rules woke her up, and to her surprise, she even learned something.

For Lucy, chemistry was a total disaster. She couldn't concentrate on formulas and found the subject dry. She had a conference with her teacher to talk about dropping the course. During their conversation, she learned that her teacher came from a small town in Indiana and had not taken chemistry in high school because she thought it was only for boys. Somehow, the personal contact with her teacher changed Lucy's perspective. Chemistry would never be her best subject, but it became more bearable. Getting to know the teacher can sometimes change your outlook on a course.

55

There are many different ways to liven up a boring class. In an English class, for instance, you might put yourself in the place of one of the characters in the novel you're reading and imagine what you would do. In a history class you might survey one aspect of the period, such as clothes, or the cooking utensils, or the water supply, and bring your expertise to class. In an economics class you might explore the question concerning investments that you've always wondered about.

Avoiding Distractions

Allowing yourself to be distracted is another way of avoiding paying attention. If you concentrate on listening, you will be surprised at how quickly noises fade into the background.

Sitting in the back of the room, daydreaming, turning off when the subject gets complicated, deciding to read your text later—all these are cop-outs. If you are really determined to get the most out of your classes, you can train yourself to be *there*, in mind as well as in body. You can learn to listen. See the chart on Tips for Good Listening.

TIPS FOR GOOD LISTENING

- Start off with a positive attitude.
- Pay attention to *how* the teacher communicates. If you are critical, think how you might do things differently.
- Listen for ideas.
- Look over yesterday's notes to remind yourself of the material that has been covered so that you'll be ready for what comes next.
- When you don't fully understand, or if you have a comment to make, raise your hand to speak, or jot down your thought to bring up later.
- Sit up front, sit up straight, look at the teacher.
- Be ready with a pencil and paper to take notes.

Listening with Pencil and Paper

Taking good notes goes hand in hand with good listening. If you want to get the most out of listening, good notes are essential.

There are five sound reasons to take notes during class. Notes help you:

- Review for tests and papers
- Focus on key points your teacher is making
- Listen actively
- Remember information
- Combat boredom, daydreaming, sleepiness

As you move from high school to college, the technique of good note taking becomes more and more important.

TIPS FOR GOOD NOTE TAKING

- Anticipate what the topic is by reading your text or yesterday's notes before you get to class.
- Have your looseleaf book open to a clean page, and be ready with pencil or pen.
- Write the class, teacher, and date at the top of the page.
- Leave wide margins on each side of your sheet for adding personal comments or emphatic points.
- Remember that the primary purpose of note taking is to record main ideas, not every word the teacher says.
- Don't waste time thinking of synonyms.

Taking Notes in Class

Certain key words your teachers use can give you the signal that important information is coming that should be jotted down.

Pay particularly close attention to your teacher's opening remarks, for they provide an overview of what the lecture is about. Focus on main points by listening for the following key words:

"Remember that . . ."
"The basic concept . . ."
"A major development . . ."
"The reason is . . ."

Listen for words that signal examples or the progression of the discussion:

"For instance . . ."
"For example . . ."
"On the other hand . . ."
"Furthermore . . ."

Concentrate on your teacher's concluding remarks. Teachers generally sum up the important points in their closing statements. By listening carefully for the key words indicating a conclusion, you are likely to pick up some of the highlights you might have missed:

"In conclusion . . ."
"Finally . . ."
"To summarize . . ."

After you have written down your notes, you must be able to read and understand them. You will have to experiment to discover what system of note taking works best for you.

Experts in the field of study skills recommend using abbreviations and symbols that you will easily understand. Some common examples:

&   and
w/   with

w/o	without
vs	against
∴	therefore
+	plus
−	minus
=	equals
<	less than
>	greater than
re	referring to, regarding

In addition, you can abbreviate words by leaving out vowels or endings. Thus the preceding sentence might be "u cn abvt wrds by lvng/o vwls & ndngs." You can also shorten sentences by eliminating words such as "the," "and," and so on. As long as you are consistent, your notes will be clear to you.

Reviewing Your Notes

Your notes are not just proof that you were present in class; they are there for you to use for review. Ideally, you should look over your notes after class, before the next class, and as part of your study before a test.

Push yourself into taking the next step: when you review your notes, question whatever seems sketchy, add whatever you can remember, and fill in the blanks by consulting your teacher, your classmates, and appropriate texts.

Studying from good class notes is similar to studying from a textbook. The more actively you are involved, the more you will get out of the process. (See the list of suggested books at the end of the chapter.)

Tackling the Text

Adam thought he studied as well as the next person. He would come home from school and do his daily assignments. His way of studying was to pick up his textbook, read the chapter through, and then close the book. Before a test he would read the chapter again, and sometimes even a third time. When his test grades came back, he was usually disappointed. "I work hard, but I'm just not a good student," he complained.

Adam didn't realize that what he needed was an effective system for getting the most out of his textbook study. In fact there does exist a recognized system, developed over the years by experts, for tackling the text.

The S Q 3R Method

S Q 3R. Is this a math formula?

It is a formula, but not a math one. S Q 3R was developed by Francis P. Robinson of Ohio State University as an aid to study that can be used by all students to improve grades. This method remains the basis for most textbook study systems and is widely recommended for college students. By using it now, in high school, you will be able to read faster, understand the material better, and fix the important points in your memory. S Q 3R stands for:

SURVEY
   QUESTION
     READ
       RECITE
       REVIEW

Survey. Before you even begin to read the assigned chapter, skim all the headings as well as the final summary paragraph. This will point up the main themes and give you a good idea of what's to come. The survey should take only a couple of minutes.

Question. Now get down to work. Asking yourself questions is the key step of this system. By looking for the answers to your questions, you will focus on the main ideas in what you're reading, have a purpose as you read along, and remember what you have read. Basically, this makes your reading a conversation with the author.

How do you ask questions? Begin by turning each heading into a question as you come to it. A heading in a history text, for example, says "The Gold Conspiracy." The first question: "What was the gold conspiracy?" You might then go on to ask: "Who was involved in the conspiracy?" Another question: "Why did it happen?" Another question: "When did it take place?"

Try asking yourself the five W's a journalist asks before writing a story: Who, What, When, Where, Why.

Read. Read to answer the question you have asked. Don't get stuck on each line. Search for the answer.

Recite. Look away from the book. *Out loud*, recite the answer to your question, using your own words. When appropriate, give an example. If you cannot answer the question, search again. Repeat the process of reciting out loud. Once you know the answer to your own question, you will understand and remember what you have read. If you do get stuck, ask yourself what it is that you don't understand and then make a note to ask your teacher about it.

Review. Once you have gone through the chapter, go back to the beginning, reread each heading, and see whether you can still answer your own questions.

This method of study, once you have become comfortable with it, is an invaluable aid to all general textbook reading and to reviewing for tests. For some subjects, like math and chemistry, you will have to add a special vocabulary. But the basic principles of S Q 3R apply to all your textbook reading. If you use S Q 3R—Survey, Question, Read, Recite, Review—you can't go wrong. You'll have a fail-proof method for learning and retaining textbook material.

Stop here and reflect on the last three chapters. Then fill out the Skills Checklist (next page). All skills can use improvement, but start honing those skills that need the most work.

SKILLS CHECKLIST				
	Nonexistent	Fair	Good	Excellent
Reading				
Comprehension				
Vocabulary				
Speed				
Writing				
Speaking				
Time Organization				
Space Organization				
Materials Organization				
Punctuality				
Listening				
Note Taking				
Text Reading				

For Your Information

Adler, Mortimer J. *How to Speak, How to Listen.* New York: Macmillan, 1983.

Pauk, Walter. *How to Study in College.* 4th ed. Boston: Houghton Mifflin, 1989.

Tchudi, Stephen. *The Young Learner's Handbook: A Guide to Solving Problems, Mastering Skills, Thinking Creatively.* New York: Macmillan, 1987.

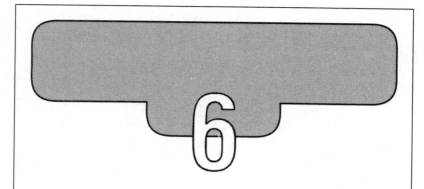

Academic
Troubleshooting

There comes a time in nearly every high school student's life when getting help with an academic problem can make the difference between barely getting by or doing well in class, between dreading or enjoying school, between just drifting through or taking charge and gaining confidence.

How do you know if you need help? Are you:

- Falling behind in schoolwork?
- Handing in homework and papers late?
- Feeling lost in class?
- Being bored in class?
- Failing tests?
- Taking on too much at once?
- Taking on too little?
- Feeling pressure most of the time?
- Having no time for outside activities?
- Feeling disorganized?
- Spinning your wheels?

If you are nodding your head, recognizing that some of these signs apply to you, you should get help. Help is there if you reach out for it.

Three Students Who Needed Help

Wayne: Getting on Track

Although he dreamed of going on to college, Wayne couldn't discuss his ambition with his classmates. In addition, he wasn't sure that the courses he was taking were the right ones to prepare him for college. He needed to talk to an adult about his future but he was afraid that no one would take him seriously.

Gathering his courage, Wayne decided to see the guidance counselor. He realized that she was the one person in the school system who would know the most about college and preparation for college.

When Wayne met with the counselor, they went over his past record and then made a preliminary schedule for the next two years. She suggested that he consider a history course in summer school to ease his future schedule, and she recommended that he speak to his English teacher for a supplementary reading list. She also steered him to several college guidebooks.

Although Wayne had been uneasy about approaching a person in authority, he was pleasantly surprised at how sympathetic the counselor was and how useful the conference turned out to be. He could see that he had a lot of work to do, but now he had a much better idea of how to get going.

Elizabeth: Losing Interest

Elizabeth's academic problems were different. All through school she had been a strong student, especially in math. At the end of her sophomore year she found that she was becoming bored. She couldn't figure out why.

It was her math teacher who noticed that she losing interest. Elizabeth had been his star student, and now her grades were slipping. He asked her to come in for a conference, and together they discovered that the math class was working on material that Elizabeth found too easy. Elizabeth wasn't being challenged. Once the problem was out in the open, the math teacher was able to suggest some possible solutions, such as taking advanced classes at the community college.

Darrell: Catching Up

Darrell had all the advantages of a big suburban high school where the majority of students were college-bound. But he spent more time with his friends than with his homework, and he hated making plans more than two hours in advance. As a result, he procrastinated so long that two English papers were overdue, and he was getting far behind in chemistry. He began to realize that he had a problem.

One day, on the way home from soccer practice, Darrell confessed to his friend Greg his worries about school. Greg said that he had been in the same situation last year, sitting in chemistry class without a clue as to what was happening. When Greg finally discussed this problem with his teacher, he was given the name of a peer tutor who helped him catch up. Things went pretty well after that.

Since Darrell had a number of academic problems, Greg advised him to get an appointment as soon as possible with his counselor to talk about school.

Darrell felt better just knowing that he was not alone. Greg had had problems like his and had gotten help. Once he had decided to make that crucial appointment with his counselor, Darrell felt relieved. He made up his mind to jot down a list of questions he wanted to discuss.

COMMON EXCUSES FOR RESISTING HELP

- Waiting too long to ask for help in the hope that things will get better by themselves
- Feeling that asking for help is a sign of weakness
- Thinking that those in authority are unapproachable
- Getting discouraged if help doesn't come through right away
- Not following through with suggestions

People Who Can Help

There are many people you can turn to for help:

- Guidance counselor
- Teacher

- Coach
- Club adviser
- Parent or relative
- Friend
- Religious leader
- Librarian
- Friend's parent
- Tutor

In determining who is the best person to approach, consider the obvious choices first. If your problem is unfocused, speak to a friend, parent, or religious leader. If you're uncertain about choices or schedules, visit the guidance office. If you're having trouble with history papers, speak to the history teacher.

Just because counselors and teachers are in authority doesn't mean that you can't approach them. Visit the guidance office at your school to make an appointment with a counselor. Approach your teacher after class and ask for an appointment, or make the request in a note left on your teacher's desk.

Counselors and teachers who have chosen to work in high schools have done so because they like to work with teenagers. Some of them may be more on your wavelength than others, but most of them will understand the problems you are going through.

Generally, teachers have a deep interest in their subject. In many cases they have gone to graduate school after college to learn more about their subject and to develop teaching skills. They want to help their students learn and to help them when something gets in the way of learning.

Counselors also have special training. In many schools counselors are classroom teachers who have returned to graduate school for special courses in the field of high school guidance. They have experience dealing with the variety of problems faced by students.

Not every student makes the right connection with his or her counselor. One possible solution is to request a change. If your school doesn't offer that option, you may have to make the best of your situation but seek advice elsewhere. Think about talking to some other people (see the list presented earlier in this section).

How to Benefit from a Conference

Good conferences don't just happen: They take practice. Your first conference may be frustrating. You may come away from it feeling that you didn't accomplish what you had intended. Perhaps the person you talked to was not quite right for your problem. Or maybe you were unable to explain what was bothering you. You may be shy about admitting the extent of your difficulties. Or you may not be clear enough about what you need advice on.

Here are some ways to improve your chances for a successful conference:

- Put your concerns in writing.
- Bring paper with you to the meeting and take notes.
- Be frank and open; don't hold back.
- Remember, you don't have to impress anyone.
- Ask questions about anything that isn't completely clear.
- Listen carefully to suggestions.
- If you have doubts about a suggestion, don't be afraid to express them.
- Be sure you make another appointment if your session didn't fully cover your problem.
- Take time after the conference to think things over.
- Check your notes.
- Follow up on suggestions.

Don't Give Up

The main point is not to give up when you're looking for help. The first person you talk to, whether it's a counselor, teacher, coach, parent, or friend, may not have all the answers. For some problems, the personality of the adviser may be of great importance. If the person doesn't seem right for you, try someone else. In other cases, the problem may be specific and what is needed is concrete, expert advice. Personality is not an important factor here.

Remember, also, that change takes time and requires patience. There are some problems you can't cure overnight. But you can, with help from the right people and with persistence, deal with the difficulties in a positive way. By seeking and getting help, you will be taking control and will be on your way to a solution.

Taking on Greater Academic Challenges

"I thought," said a college freshman, "that I could keep my mind on hold until I got to college. Actually I was afraid to compete with all the brainy people in high school, so I stayed away from anything that sounded too intellectual. I know now that I could have done more if I had tried."

Don't sell yourself short. You may be able to take on greater academic challenges. In the same way your body needs exercise to keep it in shape, so does your mind need a workout to keep it alive and well. You don't have to be 6'8" to play school yard basketball; you don't have to be a top-seed to play tennis, or an Olympic swimmer to enjoy doing laps. Yet many high school students decide that only the "geniuses" have a right to think.

Just as there are many different sports for you to get involved in, so are there many different ways to stretch your mind.

By now, having read this far, you've put yourself in the front row of the class so that you can concentrate and participate. You are listening, asking questions, and contributing to discussions. You are taking a college preparatory program that covers more than the basics. You have courses in English, history, mathematics, and science. You are studying a foreign language and continuing it for as long as your schedule and aptitude permit. You are fulfilling all the requirements for graduation, and taking physical education, art, and music as needed.

What next?

You've sparked up your class participation and expanded your interest in the world outside, but your daily academic routine still doesn't satisfy you. Perhaps you feel that your classes are moving too slowly and you think there will never be an end to the repetition. Look at chapter 4 to see if there are some cues there to liven up your experience. Even when you try out some of the suggestions, however, you may still wish for something to make the school day more interesting. When this happens, you must look into what else the school offers.

Honors Courses

Most high schools provide opportunities for students to take on greater academic challenge by offering honors courses that are more demanding versions of traditional courses. Going at a faster pace and covering additional material, these honors courses are usually livelier because they attract more involved and enthusiastic students. Having such a group of classmates is always a plus for both the students and teachers since these classes take on a special spirited quality.

"I should have taken the honors English my friends talked about," Livia said. "That course had a terrific teacher. I was bored in the regular class. I knew I could do more, but nobody expected anything from me."

Advanced Placement (AP) Courses

As part of an honors program, there may be an opportunity to take on further challenge by electing one or more Advanced Placement (AP) courses. AP courses are college-level studies in English, history, math, and science as well as the arts, language, history, economics, and government. Psychology will be added in 1991.

AP courses are designed for academically strong students eager to extend themselves. If your record indicates that you can do the work, and if you are interested in the subject, you should consider taking an AP course. Many schools have added AP courses to their curriculums with more and more students enrolled in one or more classes.

Like the honors courses, the AP classes are valuable for providing stimulating material, classmates, and teachers. And AP on a transcript usually is taken as proof that the course is rigorous.

Practical Rewards

Additionally, AP courses offer practical rewards. Students who take AP courses feel better prepared for college-level work.

In AP classes they have learned how to think critically, explore an area in depth, and write and research term papers.

After taking a special exam upon completion of each AP course, students may receive college credit and/or placement in advanced college courses. With credit earned in AP courses, a student may sometimes enter college with advanced freshman, or even sophomore, standing. Toby, for example, took AP English, AP European history, and AP French and received high grades in the AP exams. When she entered college, she opted out of the basic English course, and she received nine credits toward her college graduation requirements.

What College Admissions Counselors Say about AP

Most college admissions counselors applaud your taking AP courses. As one of them notes, "We like students to take AP courses if they are offered at their high school. They're highly desirable in a student's program because APs are quality courses."

There are, however, some caveats that the same counselors add. "Students should pursue their strengths in high school. I don't think every student should load his or her plate with spinach. You shouldn't take calculus AP if you're not a whiz," says an admissions dean.

Another counselor remarks, "Five honors or AP classes in one year are too much for most students. One or two are great, but a fifth year of a language can be just as valuable."

Packing your schedule with AP courses may limit you when it comes to taking a nontraditional class that especially interests you. Dorothy H. Dillon, writing in *The Journal of College Admissions*, says that so many schools have expanded their AP programs that "top students face increasing difficulty finding a place in their programs for the unusual course . . . for religion, philosophy, non-Western history or Japanese."

Should You Take an AP Course?

Some of you may be hesitant about trying an Advanced Placement course because you're fearful that you may not get

75

a good grade. What happens when you don't do "A" work in an Advanced Placement course? There's no one answer; it depends . . .

One college admissions officer says, "Tell us why you're getting a C in AP physics and that will help us understand your record better."

Another states, "If a student is doing very badly in an AP course, I wonder whether he or she can take on college-level work. On the other hand, if I see that a student has a superior record in the regular courses, I would want to know why that student *wasn't* taking the school's AP classes."

If your school offers AP courses and you haven't taken any, admissions officers in the selective colleges will wonder why your record lacks these classes.

Most college admissions counselors think that a B in an AP course is better than an A in an ordinary class. They know and respect the quality of the AP program and realize that not every student can get A's in every subject, especially a highly demanding one.

Many high schools, acknowledging the difficulty of such courses, give greater weight to AP (and honors) courses when they compute class standing and grade-point average. This practice may offset a lower grade.

Of course, any college is going to be interested in students who get A's in difficult courses. To be successful, you have to be willing to do the extra work that AP courses demand. You're more likely to do that if you take an AP course in a subject you enjoy. Add on additional AP courses if you can handle the work load.

Perhaps, as the term progresses, you find that you are doing C work in an AP class and question whether to go on. This is a tough call. Students who have a strong academic program and generally get good grades can afford an occasional slip. If what you're learning is sufficiently rewarding because the teacher is so good and the class so stimulating, you may decide to accept the challenge and keep at it. If that's the case, you will want to explain your grade in your interview or college application. In some high schools it may be possible to opt for a pass/fail grade so that the mark doesn't affect your record, but don't take this route as a dodge to escape the work. College admissions counselors may wonder why you chose this option.

Deciding whether to take one or more AP courses is a question you have to answer for yourself. With the help of people who know you and the school situation, you should strive for a sensible equation that balances your interests, abilities, and ambition.

The International Baccalaureate

In addition to AP programs, some schools offer other special programs for doing advanced work. A few sponsor an International Baccalaureate program and diploma in which students take courses in math, experimental science, social studies, language, and an elective using curriculum guidelines and exams established by an international committee. Also included is an interdisciplinary course on the philosophy of learning that stimulates students to reflect critically on the knowledge and experience acquired in and outside the classroom.

The idea behind the program is to offer an integrated liberal approach to education that is complemented by the opportunity to study a subject in depth. The IB diploma is recognized as an international academic passport of high intellectual achievement. (An address for this program is listed at the end of the chapter.)

When Your High School Has No Advanced Program

Some high schools do not provide a specific program for students who want to take on greater academic challenges. Should you find yourself in this position, it is important that you talk to your guidance counselor or a teacher who can help you locate outside resources.

For example, when Elizabeth's math teacher found that she was losing interest because the work in class was not up to her level, he suggested that she take an advanced math course in the community college the following year. Elizabeth had not known that taking a college-level course was possible, and the idea really intrigued her. Her teacher also encouraged her to concentrate on qualifying for the countywide math team.

Internships, Independent Study, and Other Possibilities

Your teachers, counselor, and parents may be urging you to take honors, AP, or even IB classes, if offered. You, on the other hand, are torn between taking on such a vigorous work load and doing other projects of great interest to you.

You may be so captivated by medical research, for instance, that you have found an internship program that takes you out of the classroom and into a hospital operating room. One high school offers an "executive internship" program to students who work as assistants-in-training in county or federal agencies and hospitals. Other internships offer a variety of placements in business fields, theater groups, TV and radio stations.

Or you may be able to do independent work under the supervision of a teacher in your school. Sandy, with the help of his history and English teachers, took on a study of his town's architectural history. Sue, in a school where advanced Latin wasn't offered, found that she could take a correspondence course under supervision through her state university.

You might, like Maria, find that another high school offers more intensive courses in your field of interest. Maria arranged her program so that she could spend afternoons in a school with an outstanding studio art course. Annie went to a different high school to take Russian, and Joe went to another school for AP physics.

In most areas the local community college offers high school students an opportunity to take classes in subjects that their own high schools do not have. Some high schools even allow students to earn both high school and college credit by taking courses in an area college. Luke, a math whiz, had taken every math course his high school offered, but he wanted to study even further before college. With his counselor's help, he enrolled in an advanced math course at his nearby state university.

If you have gone beyond the curriculum in your high school and want to pursue a subject, investigate courses in nearby colleges to find out if you can fit them into your program.

Developing Special Talents

There are some students who are exceptionally talented in a particular field. It is especially important that these students utilize the facilities of the school system to enhance their capabilities. Taking the most challenging courses in school is one route. Attending a magnet school that specializes in a particular field might be the way to go. Finding outside challenges is still another route.

Mark and Denise were both encouraged by their science teacher to develop projects for the Westinghouse Science Search. Barbara and Jason, talented writers, were persuaded to look into the National Endowment for the Humanities Young Scholars Program that funds high school (and college) students for a summer's research thesis on a humanities-related subject. Both these programs are open to interested, committed students. In both programs having the support of a teacher or mentor is important to qualify.

In addition, there are summer programs especially geared for specific talents (see chapter 10).

Challenging Yourself

No student has to wait until college to go beyond the ordinary high school curriculum. As we have seen in this chapter, you have a wide variety of options:

- Advanced courses
- Independent projects

- Special research
- Courses at other high schools
- Courses at a community or four-year college
- Correspondence courses
- Internships

The opportunities are there for you to explore and enjoy and learn. Challenge yourself!

For Your Information

Publications

Deutschman, Alan. *Winning Money for College: The High School Student's Guide to Scholarship Contests*. Princeton: Peterson's Guides, 1987.

Feingold, S. Norman, and Marie Feingold, *Scholarships, Fellowships. and Loans*. Vol. 8, Bethesda, Md.: Bellman Publishing, 1987.

Science Service. *Directory of Science Training Programs for High Ability Students*. Washington, D.C.: Science Service, Annual.

Organizations

Advanced Placement Program
The College Board
Princeton, N.J. 08541-6670

International Baccalaureate North America
200 Madison Avenue
Room 2043
New York, N.Y. 10016

National Endowment for the Humanities
Younger Scholars Awards
Division of Fellowships and Seminars
1100 Pennsylvania Avenue
Washington, D.C. 20506

Westinghouse Science Talent Search
Science Service, Inc.
1719 N Street, N.W.
Washington, D.C. 20036

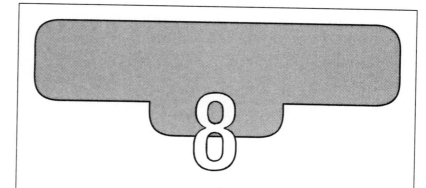

Help!
I Need Somebody!
Coping with
Special Problems

"We talk about it sometimes after school," said Greg, "about how we can feel on top of the world one day and down in the dumps the day after. Everybody's got a different problem—with friends, sex, parents, grades. We all feel the pressure."

These pressures, along with the prevalence of drinking and drugs, confront teenagers in a complex world. High school students face them on a daily basis, and most manage to make positive choices for themselves.

"It was hard," said Chuck. "I had to break away from the crowd I'd been hanging around with since junior high. But it was that or go along with the drinking."

Resisting peer pressure and facing up to other common strains is tough. Many schools, recognizing that they have to find ways to help students cope, have launched programs that actively address these concerns.

There are other situations, however, that are special because most students don't face them. Examples include moving to a new school or having to work long hours at a job to help support the family. These situations are not catastrophes, but they can be upsetting, some more so than others. They are predicaments imposed from the outside. The student cannot change the basic situation but rather must find a way to make the best of it.

Moving to a New School

Moving from one town to another affects people differently. Some may be excited and thrive on the new move, but others may be worried and upset.

Because Kay's father was in the foreign service, her family was accustomed to moving from place to place. By the time she was 16, Kay had lived in three different countries and now was transferring to a suburban high school in the United States. She was a little scared but mainly enthusiastic about entering a regular American high school.

83

Rob's father worked for a company that was about to move its headquarters from New York City to Dallas. Rob was devastated at the thought of leaving his old neighborhood and his team in the middle of the basketball season.

Tiffany had just discovered a new group of friends when her mother told her that because of the divorce they would be moving to another town. She was convinced that her new school would be snobbish and full of cliques that would never let her in.

Like other students who find themselves in this situation, Kay, Rob, and Tiffany had to go through two main stages in the moving process:

- Saying good-bye to the old school
- Getting settled in the new school

Neither part is easy. But brooding, being angry, blaming parents, and deciding there's nothing you can do except to run away will only make the whole process more difficult.

Taking an active role in the two stages of the moving process will ease the strain not only on yourself but also on your family. Here are some suggestions for what you *can* do:

Leaving

- Face up to good-byes: to places, to friends. Slipping away may seem easier, but if you make a point of saying good-bye, you will be comforted later by memories of the leave-taking.
- Plan to keep in touch with your friends—by letter, by telephone, by an occasional visit if you will live near enough to return.
- Don't wait for an invitation to a farewell party; take the initiative and throw one for yourself.
- Go easy on your schoolmates and family. Your friends may say the wrong thing when they mean to tell you they will

miss you. Your family may seem irritable and insensitive to your distress when they mean only to say that they are having trouble too.

- Negotiate in a reasonable way with your parents. They may not know how much it means to you to stay behind for a prom or a track meet. Sometimes it is possible, with planning, to arrange to live temporarily with a school-mate, relative, or family friend.
- Meet with your guidance counselor and talk to your teachers as far in advance of the move as possible. Not only will they need to transfer your records, but they may also have ideas and suggestions about how to make the transition easier both academically and socially.

Setting In

- Give yourself time. Remember that there's no such thing as an instant transition. Everything will be strange until, gradually, people and places become familiar.
- Check out academic requirements. Be frank with teachers about differences between your old school and your new school in methods of teaching and content of courses. Let them help you catch up or go ahead in specific areas.
- Be open and friendly. People will be curious about you. They will approach you if you don't push them away. Making new friends doesn't mean you are deserting the old ones.
- Join at least one club or activity that interests you. There's nothing that brings people together more quickly than working or playing at something they all enjoy.
- Accentuate the positive: moving to a new school can make good changes in life. You can shed your old image as class clown, bookworm, or loner. You can get rid of an old nickname you've always hated. You can start out with a new style of hair or clothes or attitude that you've always wanted to try. You can change the kinds of friends you may

have outgrown. You can rearrange your room, your relationship with your family, your view of yourself. It's a fresh start.

Having to Work

In contrast to those students who work to earn pocket money, many students must work after school to contribute to the family support. These students have no choice. Working after school while keeping up with studies isn't easy. For those who must work every day and on weekends and still maintain decent grades in school, organization is the key (see chapter 4).

Ralph was one of many children in a single-parent household, and he had to supplement his mother's income by earning as much money on a job as possible.

Troy's family didn't have the income to afford college fees, so he had to find a job that would enable him to save up for tuition.

Janet's mother had been forced to stop work in order to stay home and care for Janet's younger brother. Janet had to help out the family by taking a job.

The exacting schedule of work and school made hard demands on all three students. Ralph, Troy, and Janet had to establish good study habits in order to get their homework done, write papers, study for tests, and also find time to be with their friends. They couldn't even think about joining any after-school activities.

Ralph's job search led him to the fast-food franchise close to home. This saved him travel time and carfare, both of which were important to him.

In investigating jobs, Troy found that most part-time work paid no more than the minimum wage. He knew he could get a job as a bagger in the supermarket, but he was hoping for something more interesting. He thought he would really like to work at the local radio station where he could find out more about sports announcing, but when he applied at the personnel office he was told there were no positions open.

He took the job as a bagger, but he went back to the station once a month to see if something had turned up. When summer came and an opening developed for a "go-fer"—someone to run errands and do other general chores—the personnel manager remembered Troy and offered him the job. He stayed there for the rest of his high school years, gaining valuable experience *and* a great college recommendation from the station manager.

Janet couldn't find a single part-time job that offered enough hours of work to provide her with a sufficient income. After considerable searching, she managed to find two jobs that fit her schedule—one at a plant nursery and one at a department store. Gradually, she became more and more interested in plants, trees, and other aspects of horticulture. In spring the nursery offered her an expanded schedule; she was able to give up the salesclerk job and to work exclusively at what she loved and what promised to develop into a lifelong career.

All three had to work after school, sacrificing extracurricular school activities that would have steered them into worthwhile experiences. Troy and Janet managed to find jobs that kindled their individual interests, giving them a good start on their future careers.

If you have to work after school, try to find something you're interested in doing. It makes sense for now and in your future. This is not always possible, but it is worth a try.

Family Problems

All families have ups and downs, good times and angry times. At one moment you may think you have the greatest parents in the world; at another moment you may wish you had been born to a completely different set of parents. Sisters and brothers usually don't behave exactly the way you would like them to.

In addition, you and your parents may have ongoing conflicts: curfews and privacy, chores and responsibilities, allowances and part-time work, freedom and independence. Part of growing up is recognizing that all of this is normal and requires negotiation (see chapter 4).

Other family problems, however, are more severe.

Jane's mother, for example, was in and out of the hospital for cancer treatments. Jane was frightened for her mother and felt responsible for her father and her younger sister.

Glenn knew that his older brother was into drugs. His parents didn't seem to want to deal with it. He was tormented over what to do.

Lucy's father drank too much and yelled and threw things when he wasn't sober. Sometimes it got so bad she just felt like running away.

Margarite's parents had been fighting for years and finally decided to get a divorce. In a way it was a relief, but she couldn't stand the way each one was bad-mouthing the other and tugging at her. She felt confused and guilty all the time.

Severe family problems can include many other situations such as physical or sexual abuse, a sick brother or sister who needs constant care, death of a parent.

Sometimes several problems come all at once, with worries about money adding to the distress.

Look to People for Help

No high school student should expect to handle severe problems such as these alone. There is no need to suffer in silence. Reaching out for help is the right thing to do.

Ordinarily you would turn to a parent. But in many cases, that is not possible. Where else can you go?

Think of your extended family: a grandparent, aunt or uncle or cousin may be hesitant about interfering but may very well be waiting for you to call. You may be comfortable talking to a neighbor or the parent of a friend. Consider speaking to a religious leader, even if you haven't been active in your place of worship. Perhaps there is a counselor, teacher, or family doctor to whom you can turn.

Other Places to Look for Help

It may be, however, that right now you are not ready to discuss your family problem with anyone.

Lucy, for example, was so upset by her father's drunken behavior that her schoolwork suffered and her social life was almost nonexistent. Her mother acted as if nothing was wrong, and her father was unreachable. She was too embarrassed to tell anyone about what went on in her house.

Unable to do any schoolwork at home, she took refuge in the library. While she was browsing in the stacks one day, she came across a book for teenagers about alcoholic parents. Reading this first book helped Lucy see a way out. It steered her to further resources and people, and she no longer felt helpless and alone.

Library Resources

If, like Lucy, you have a family problem and do not yet feel comfortable talking to anyone about it, the library is a good place to start your search for help. In addition to books, the public library usually has a bulletin board of current flyers and pamphlets with information, addresses, and telephone numbers of groups that deal with a great variety of family problems.

Librarians in the information, reference, or teenage division are good consultants. You can ask them for resource material without directly discussing your problem.

The reference division may have a directory of community organizations offering outreach services. The white and yellow pages of the phone book are also a good resource; check under Hotline, Alateen, Al-Anon, United Way, and the Social Service heading for numbers to call.

In addition, you can look up the subject that characterizes

your situation (such as alcoholism, divorce, drug abuse, eating disorders, mental illness) in the card catalog or computerized file in your library.

Through books and other library materials, you will discover that many other young people have gone through what you are now experiencing; they have felt helpless, guilty, angry, ashamed, overly responsible, and overwhelmed. You are not alone.

Hotlines

Failing in school, breaking up with a boyfriend or girlfriend, experiencing the shock of divorce or death in the family can be the last straw for someone already troubled. Problems are overwhelming, and there seems to be no way out.

If you are distraught and in need of immediate help, head straight for the hotline. You will find the number in the phone book or through the information operator. Hotline people are trained to give help over the phone without asking for your name or being intrusive. Some hotlines include specialists in teenage problems. Talking over your situation with a sympathetic, knowledgeable person can steady you and ease your distress.

Many young people may feel despair at one time or another. Some, however, feel so desperate that their thoughts turn to suicide. If this is the case for you or a friend, you *must* confide in an adult. There is a whole network of people who can help. The hotline people will respect the seriousness of your distress and will provide immediate, confidential attention. All the resources listed in this chapter, including friends, family, and social services, can help you and guide you to a caring professional. Remember, as terrible as things seem, suicide is a permanent solution to a temporary problem.

You *Can* Do Something about Your Problem

There is no way that this book can deal with every crisis that comes up in a high school student's life. Growing up isn't easy; even under the best of circumstances, there will be crises to face during these high school years. But keep in mind that no matter what your problem, there are books, organizations, and people to help you cope. (See For Your Information below for additional suggestions.) You should not suffer in silence. You are doing the right thing when you reach out for help.

For Your Information

Anorexia and Bulimia

Landau, Elaine. *Why Are They Starving Themselves? Understanding Anorexia Nervosa and Bulimia.* New York: Julian Messner, 1983.

Child Abuse

Hyde, Margaret O. *Sexual Abuse: Let's Talk about It.* Rev. and enl. ed. Philadelphia: Westminster Press, 1987.

National Center on Child Abuse and Neglect
Children's Bureau
U.S. Department of Health and Human Services
Box 1182
Washington, D.C. 20013

National Child Abuse Coalition
1125 15th Street N.W.
Suite 300
Washington, D.C. 20005

Death or Illness in the Family

Fine, Judylaine. *Afraid to Ask: A Book for Families to Share about Cancer.* New York: Lothrop, Lee and Shepard Books, 1986.
LeShan, Eda. *Learning to Say Good-bye: When A Parent Dies.* New York: Macmillan, 1976.
Richter, Elizabeth. *Losing Someone You Love: When a Brother or Sister Dies.* New York: Putnam's, 1986.

Divorce and Step-Families

Craven, Linda. *Step-Families: New Patterns in Harmony.* New York: Julian Messner, 1982.
Krementz, Jill. *How It Feels When Parents Divorce.* New York: Knopf, 1984.

Robson, Bonnie, M.D. *My Parents Are Divorced, Too: Teenagers Talk about Their Experiences and How They Cope.* New York: Everest House, 1980.

Moving

Nida, Patricia Cooney, Ph.D., and Wendy M. Heller. *The Teenager's Survival Guide to Moving.* New York: Atheneum, 1985.

Substance Abuse

Cohen, Daniel, and Susan Cohen. *A Six-Pack and a Fake I.D.: Teens Look at the Drinking Question.* New York: M. Evans, 1986.

Hyde, Margaret O., editor. *Mind Drugs.* New York: McGraw-Hill, 1981.

Ryerson, Eric. *When Your Parent Drinks Too Much: A Book for Teenagers.* New York: Facts on File Publications, 1985.

Alateen and Al-Anon groups are listed in the white pages of the phone book. Or you can write to:

Al-Anon Family Group Headquarters
Box 182 Madison Square Station
New York, N.Y. 10159

National Clearinghouse for Alcohol Information
Box 2345
Rockville, MD 20852

Suicide

Leder, Jane Mersky. *Dead Serious: A Book for Teenagers about Teenage Suicide.* New York: Atheneum, 1987.

Teen Problems

Cohen, Susan, and Daniel Cohen. *Teenage Competition: A Survival Guide.* New York: M. Evans, 1987.

Glenbard East Echo staff. Howard Spanogla, editor. *Teenagers Themselves.* New York: Adama Books, 1984, 1988.

Rinzler, Jane. *Teens Speak Out: A Report from Today's Teens on Their Most Intimate Thoughts, Feelings, and Hopes for the Future.* New York: Donald I. Fine, 1986.

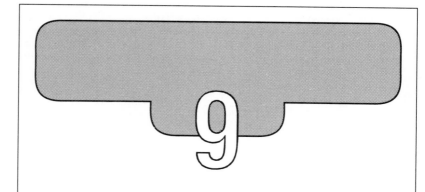

9

Beyond the Classroom: Participating in Extracurricular Activities

Emma's Choice: A Dramatic Situation

Emma was looking for a way to meet some new people outside of class. Her friend Kim invited her to come along to the first meeting of the drama club. "But, I'm not an actress!" Emma protested.

Kim told her that the club already had enough actresses. What was needed were people who were willing to help with scenery and props and lighting and a hundred other backstage jobs.

Joining the stage crew turned out to be just right for Emma. She liked learning the backstage skills and especially enjoyed working on a production with a lively bunch of new people. "It was a great feeling—going through the ups and downs and then seeing the whole thing come together on opening night in May. We really had something to celebrate!"

Extracurricular activity can make a big difference in your life as well. It can brighten your days and open up possibilities by giving you:

- An active role to play
- New friendships
- The opportunity to use untapped talents
- A welcome change from the classroom routine

Laurie and Bruce: Newspaper Duo

Laurie, who did layout for the school newspaper, and Bruce, who sold ads, agreed that holding a tangible product in their hands at the end of every week made them proud. It was not like getting a good mark on a test. Nobody was forcing them to work hard; nobody was grading them. Except for the general guidance of their adviser, they were on their own.

"We know how much work we've put in and if we've done our best," said Laurie. "We don't need anybody bugging us. We make mistakes, but we learn something new every time we put out the paper."

Extracurricular activity gave Laurie and Bruce:

- Positive feedback
- Independent thinking
- Responsibility
- Opportunity for creativity
- A chance to learn from mistakes

Carl: Time Out for Soccer

Carl's life after school was spent mostly on the soccer field. He had not made the school varsity team, which was a crushing disappointment. But he swallowed his pride and, at the suggestion of the school coach, joined the community recreational team. He was also doing some coaching himself—helping out with the neighborhood league for 7- to 9-year-olds.

When Carl's parents asked him whether he was spending too much time away from the books, he responded: "Being outdoors and playing hard clears my head. I can't sit so much. I need to move, to be doing something. And I like the teaching part too. When my kids learn to kick the ball in the right direction, I feel great!"

Extracurricular activity gave Carl:

- A change from physical passivity to physical activity
- Competitive experience
- Cooperative experience
- A chance to try out different abilities
- Practice in leadership

Extracurricular Dividends

There are even more reasons to look beyond the classroom into extracurriculars. Recent studies by the Department of Education have revealed that good grades and extracurricular activities tend to go together. The study also noted that involved students were likely to take more, rather than fewer, academic courses.

Most high schools have an array of extracurricular activities, ranging from athletics to writing, from social clubs to service clubs, from band to debate. As Emma, Laurie, Bruce, and Carl discovered, there are many different ways of participating. You don't have to be a star performer in the musical, the editor of the newspaper, or the president of the Student Government Association to gain pleasure and satisfaction from activities.

Don't Take on Too Much

Remember, however, that extracurricular activities will no longer be pleasurable if you take on more than you can handle. Don't fall into the traps of overscheduling activities, taking activities for the wrong reasons, or overdoing a single activity.

Simon: Too Many Activities

Simon didn't need to be encouraged to jump into after-school activities. As a freshman, he took up every activity in sight. He went out for track; he played trumpet in the marching band; he was elected delegate to the student government; and, on top of all that, he thought he could become the star of the debate team.

Fortunately, Simon found out before disaster struck that he could not manage all the activities that excited him and still go to class and do his homework. In his sophomore year, he decided to stick with track and debate.

Nancy: Joining for the Wrong Reasons

Nancy, on the other hand, had concentrated on peer counseling as her only extracurricular activity in her freshman and sophomore years. As a junior, she began to worry about her college applications. All at once she rushed to join the yearbook staff, the student government, and the prom committee; she became a member of Students Against Driving Drunk (SADD), went out for the tennis team, and volunteered for the homeless drive.

"What," her counselor asked, "is going on here? Why all the sudden activity?"

Nancy admitted to worrying about having very little to put down on her activities record. She didn't think peer counseling was enough, and she was afraid the empty spaces on her college applications would be held against her.

Her counselor assured her that admissions people were experienced enough to see through "brownie points" accumulated solely for the sake of college. "What you should do is concentrate on your real interest. If that's peer counseling, go with it. Devote more time to it, if you like, but don't get involved with a bunch of thises and thats that have nothing much to do with you."

Tony: Getting Carried Away with One Activity

Tony's problem was not that he took on too many activities but that he was overly involved with one. Seeded number one on the tennis team, Tony had a wicked serve and was developing a backhand slice that won point after point. As his tennis game improved, he found himself spending more and more time on the court—taking lessons, practicing, playing on the school team, entering competitions and tournaments. His coach was prodding him to devote even more hours to workouts.

Tony began to feel too pressured. His schoolwork was suffering. He talked out his situation with parents and friends, and came to the conclusion that tennis was not going to be his whole life. He had other ambitions, and he knew that without total commitment to the sport he could not reach the top. He recognized that certain colleges would seek him out for the team, but he couldn't make it to the college of his choice on tennis alone. As the reality of this set in, Tony decided that he needed to settle down and hit the books.

Volunteer Work

Many students in high school feel cut off from the world outside. You yourself may have felt restless, full of vitality, but with no place to put your energy. You have a need to be connected to a life beyond history classes and football games. Volunteering for community service is one way to make this connection.

"Once you do it," Steffi said, "you love it." She was talking about helping out in a home for the elderly.

"When they call me 'Mister,' it makes me feel important. It shows they respect me, and I like that," said Dwight. He was talking about tutoring neighborhood kids who were potential dropouts. "I wish I'd had somebody like me to look up to when I was in elementary school."

"You learn to feel for people. Helping out gives me a lot of satisfaction." David was talking about distributing food to the homeless at a soup kitchen.

Volunteering can give you:

- A sense of purpose
- The satisfaction of helping others
- The discovery that you have much to offer
- The experience of taking charge
- Relief from school competitiveness
- An understanding of people in different age groups, economic situations, cultures

In addition, community service can provide important opportunities for career exploration and work experience. You may choose to work in a hospital, an elementary school, a program for the handicapped. You can volunteer for any of these positions:

- Tutor
- Candy Striper at the hospital
- Aide for the elderly
- Aide in the Emergency Room
- Aide at the Fire Department
- Paramedic on a rescue squad
- Nursing-home aide
- Reader for the blind
- Special Olympics aide
- Aide for the handicapped
- Worker at a soup kitchen
- Big Brother, Big Sister

Any of these activities, and many others, will give you a glimpse into careers you might want to think about later.

Paid Part-Time Work

In the beginning, Theresa loved putting on the orange uniform of the fast-food franchise she worked at weekends and two afternoons a week. She liked getting to know her co-workers and learning how to deal with people. She especially liked the money she earned that paid for extras.

Some experts say that working helps a teenager become a self-reliant adult. They believe that part-time work encourages responsibility and self-discipline and can give students good experience in working with others as well as in organizing spare time.

Others disagree. They contend that the low-level jobs most high school students get are unsatisfying and teach them to dislike work. They argue that working part-time simply to earn money for luxuries is "buying distractions from education." These people believe that students who work long hours after school tend to do less homework, to bypass tough classes, and to end up with no time for the extracurricular activities that help develop responsible participation. One counselor said, "Students who work for gadgets and luxuries are majoring in shopping when they should be studying."

Is This Job Necessary?

After Theresa had spent a couple of months flipping hamburgers and scooping out french fries, the novelty began to wear off.

"I got sick of it," she told her friend. "It turned out to be really boring, and it made me tired."

Did Theresa really need to work after school?

When she thought about it, she realized that her allowance was enough to pay for basics. She was using her earned money for frills and trinkets that were nice, but not nice enough to compensate for the time she was giving up.

"I hardly had a chance to eat dinner with my family. I didn't have time to talk to my friends, and I couldn't get to field hockey practice after school."

Fred had another problem. He had fallen into the "car trap." His job as a busboy at a country club 10 miles from his home required that he have his own transportation or else be driven back and forth by someone in the family. He talked his parents into financing a used car, with the promise that he would repay them from earnings. He had not calculated the cost of running the car: license, gas, frequent repairs. He ended up working just to keep up the car.

"Secretly," he admitted later, "it was the car I wanted when I chose that job. I didn't realize what a pain it was going to be, and how the whole thing would take up all my spare time and money."

If you are working at a part-time job that doesn't contribute to family support but merely satisfies a craving for luxury items, you should consider whether the job is really necessary. At the very least, you should put a limit on the number of working hours. When you stand behind a counter or balance trays 20 hours a week simply to earn money for designer-label clothes or car repairs, you are giving up valuable study and extracurricular time. It makes no sense.

Earning Alternatives

Some students have found better ways to earn money than flipping hamburgers or pumping gas, both jobs that tied them down to a set number of hours. Babysitting and mowing lawns, for instance, have the advantage of allowing you to be in charge of your own time. You aren't restricted to a rigid schedule.

There are other after-school jobs that offer career experience or a chance to try something creative. Charlie, for instance, found he could earn money and at the same time fill a need in his community by shopping for elderly shut-ins. "I felt good about what I was doing. And besides, I heard a lot of interesting stories. I even used one of them for a theme I wrote for English."

Ellen loved clowning around and discovered she could earn money by entertaining at kids' birthday parties. Zack and Alison pooled their cooking talents and were hired by their parents' friends to cater dinner parties. Arnie developed a reputation as the neighborhood handyman who could fix anything, and Lorenzo as the community artist who could design posters and invitations. All of them were using their talents, making their own schedules, and earning money besides.

An Enriching Experience

When you're in high school, the classroom is pretty much the center of your life. What you do outside the classroom—extracurricular, volunteer, paid work—can enrich your high school experience. Opportunity is out there. Look it over and discover what is best for you. But keep in mind that your highest priority is school. You want to enrich that in-school experience with after-school activities that help you build confidence in yourself and your abilities.

EXTRACURRICULAR ACTIVITIES CHECKLIST

Here are some activities your school or community may offer. Check off those in which you have been participating. Circle those you have not thought of or have postponed doing. Make sure you fit in those that interest you most before you graduate.

Art
  Ceramics ☐
  Fashion ☐
  Film ☐
  Graphics ☐
  Photography ☐
  Studio ☐
  Other ☐

Athletics _____
        (sport)
  Intramural ☐
  Community ☐
  Recreation ☐
  Junior varsity ☐
  Varsity ☐
Civic Affairs ☐
Community Service ☐
Dance ☐
Debating ☐
Drama or Theater ☐
Ethnic or Cross-Cultural
  Activity ☐
Foreign Exchange or
  Study Abroad ☐
Foreign Language ☐
Forensics ☐

Journalism ☐
Literary Activity ☐
Math or Computer Activity
  ☐
Music
  Instrumental ☐
  Vocal ☐
Outdoor Interests ☐
Politics ☐
Religion ☐
Science ☐
Cheerleading/Drill Team ☐
Student Government ☐
TV or Radio ☐
Volunteer Work ☐
Work ☐

Clubs _____

_____

Other Activities _____

_____

Other Interests _____

_____

For Your Information

Bureau of Labor Statistics, U.S. Department of Labor. *Occupational Outlook Handbook*. Washington, D.C.: U.S. Government Printing Office. Annual.

Feingold, S. Norman, and Shirley Levin. *What to Do until the Counselor Comes: A Handbook for Educational, Vocational, and Career Planning*. Rev. ed. New York: Rosen Publishing Group, 1983.

Harrison, Charles H. *Student Service: The New Carnegie Unit*. Princeton, N.J.: Carnegie Foundation for the Advancement of Teaching, 1987.

Lobb, Charlotte. *Exploring Apprenticeship Careers*. New York: Richards Rosen Press, 1982.

10

Using Summers for Earning and Learning

Paul spent the summer working at McDonald's, swimming, and hanging out with friends. He had a pretty good time, but at the end of the eight weeks he didn't feel he had accomplished much. He wanted to do something more interesting next summer—something like what Frank had done.

Frank, interested in science, had explored several different prospects months before the school year ended. He had landed a job at the National Institutes of Health lab outside Washington, D.C., but he needed to find a place to live. Luckily, his mother had a cousin who was happy to put him up. The work assigned to Frank turned out to be fairly routine—washing bottles, sorting slides—but the research scientists, sensing his enthusiasm, allowed him to sit in on some of their meetings. He began to understand how scientists think and how much painstaking detail goes into their work. He was awed by their quick minds and wild humor. He hoped, one day, to be one of them.

An Ideal Time

Summer is the ideal time to look beyond the classroom. It is a time when you can continue with the after-school activities you've already begun, or you can embark on something entirely different. You can strengthen an interest or venture into unknown territory.

With this big chunk of unscheduled time to play with, you can use the summer to experiment and explore. Summers give you a break from your daily routine. Of course, demands are still made on your time. You may have to earn money for necessities; you may have to go to summer school to make up a class. But even with such restrictions, there's time for a summer activity of your own choosing.

Throughout the school year you've been a prisoner of schedules, timetables, programs. In the summer you have a chance to free yourself from the routine pressure. You can:

- Be free of daily school pressure
- Take programs unavailable at other times

- Change your environment
- Expand a current interest
- Discover a new interest
- Improve a talent
- Meet new people
- Take on a challenge
- Become more independent
- Invest in your own future

Dreams of Summer

Tim yearned for forests and mountains. Barbara wished she could learn more about politics, Jason about stocks and bonds. Brian wanted to move ahead academically so that he could graduate early. Eileen craved the excitement of the theater. Marty, Arthur, and Julie recognized that they each needed money to fund their dreams: Marty to start a compact disc collection, Arthur to fix up his car, and Julie to save for college. Bianca wanted to use her photographic talent. Beth's dream was to ride horses in the country for hours on end. Will wanted to speak Spanish fluently. André wished he could make movies. Katy didn't know what interested her and wished she did. Barry dreamed of becoming a writer. Jesse thought he would enjoy the orchestra more if he could move from second fiddle to first chair. Jenny wanted to be part of a community effort. Ken wanted to try out hospital work.

Designing Your Own Summer

Most students find that summer plans work out better when they think about options and make their own choices. A good way to start is to make your own wish list.

The wish list on the next page just touches on the variety of available options. Use anything that interests you as a key to open up summer possibilities.

Wish List

I wish I could travel to _____.

I wish I could have some outdoor adventure

    biking _____ hiking _____ rafting _____ camping _____

    climbing _____ other _____.

I wish I could become better at

    music _____ art _____ drama _____ writing _____

    photography _____ tennis _____ soccer _____

    swimming _____ basketball _____ other _____.

I wish I could learn a new skill

    sewing _____ cooking _____ baking _____ carpentry _____

    jewelry designing _____ repairing bikes _____

    watch repairing _____ other _____.

I wish I could be useful by

    working in a hospital _____ tutoring _____

    helping in an underdeveloped country _____

    doing a community service project _____ other _____.

I wish I could see what it's like to be a

    doctor _____ lawyer _____ engineer _____

    teacher_____ computer specialist _____ sports

    announcer_____ journalist _____ architect _____

    farmer _____ teacher _____ politician _____ TV

    announcer _____ psychologist _____ builder _____

    business manager _____ stockbroker _____ fashion

    designer _____ chef _____ veterinarian _____ other _____.

Ways to Make Wishes Come True

There's more than one way to fulfill a wish. Tim, who yearned for forests and mountains, could:

- Join a hostel group
- Take on an Outward Bound adventure
- Join a local hike/bike group
- Go to an outdoor camp
- Work at a wilderness camp
- Work on a farm
- Work for the National Park Service
- Join the Youth Conservation Corps
- Continue Boy Scout activities

Bianca the photographer, André the potential moviemaker, Barry the writer, Jesse the musician, and Barbara the aspiring politician all wanted to improve a skill or learn a new one. They could:

- Take a summer course at a high school or college
- Enroll in a program at a museum
- Go to a specialized art, music, science, or sports camp
- Volunteer, apprentice, or intern in their area of interest

Jenny and Ken wanted to do community service. They could:

- Contact a service agency such as the Red Cross or YES (Youth Engaged in Service to America) regional office
- Explore local possibilities such as soup kitchens, hospitals, child care facilities, senior citizen homes
- Devise a project to fulfill a need in the community
- Investigate overseas assistance projects
- Consult a teacher, counselor, religious leader for other ideas

Katy finally decided she wanted to travel. She could:

- Be a foreign exchange student at an overseas high school
- Live with a foreign family
- Volunteer for a work program abroad
- Travel with a teen group
- Enroll in a foreign university course for high school students

Practical Considerations

Of course, there is also the practical side to consider. Hilary needed to take a chemistry course. She could:

- Check out summer courses at her high school
- Explore programs at local or out-of-town prep schools
- Inquire about community college classes
- Investigate college campus courses

Janet needed to earn money. She could:

- Become familiar with job-hunting techniques such as making telephone inquiries, writing resumes, interviewing
- Check the job postings on her school's bulletin board
- Spread the word among friends, relatives, teachers
- Talk to her guidance counselor
- Seek advice from a librarian on work-related pamphlets and books
- Read the want ads in the newspaper for ideas and opportunities
- Contact her local or state employment agency
- Investigate federal programs for teenagers
- Check out job subjects in the yellow pages of the phone book

A Flexible Approach Pays Off

There are ways of combining wishes, dreams, and practical considerations. Being flexible in your approach to summer wishes and obligations increases your chances for success and enjoyment.

You may not be able to wholly finance the trip of your dreams. But you can look into exchange programs and scholarships. Another alternative is to work part of the summer and travel part of the summer.

You may have to make up some academic requirements in summer school. But that needn't take the whole day or the whole summer. You have some choice in what you do with the rest of the time, and where you take the course.

You may have to work to help out your family. But nobody says the only summer job is in a fast-food restaurant or a gas station. With planning, you may find a job that pays as well and that is more productive and interesting.

Whatever it is that you are thinking of doing for the summer, remember that there is not just one way to make it happen. You can include studying and working; earning money and gaining experience; concentrating on one activity or combining activities; living at home or away from home.

Planning: The Key to Summer Success

"I couldn't decide what I wanted to do with the summer and I didn't want to deal with the problem. So I let it go 'til June. I ended up: (a) lifeguarding, (b) pumping gas, (c) waitressing."

Take your choice, provided it is a choice. Maybe you've decided that one of the above is your dream for the summer. But more likely you have, like many people, simply let things go until there was *no* choice and you had to take whatever came along.

Planning takes practice. Some people do it more naturally

than others. But it is an important skill to learn during your high school years. You can be your own fairy godmother, creating for yourself the kind of "luck" that always seems to happen to other people.

Suppose you are thinking of a wilderness adventure, a research internship, an overseas or state-sponsored program, or a job that pays well. Early planning gives you more options. You also have the time to explore possibilities thoroughly, to seek out resource books and people who are in the know.

Once you have narrowed your choices, you can apply in time to make deadlines. Many programs have deadlines, and if you don't meet them, you give up a good opportunity. Applying early—being first in line—gives you an edge.

By giving yourself time to investigate the program or job you are interested in, you can see if it is likely to live up to your expectations. Some openings that sound good on paper turn out to be disappointing in reality. Beth, for instance, wanted to combine her love of horses with her need to earn some money. At the last minute, she saw an ad in a magazine for someone to assist on a horse farm. She was so excited that she didn't bother to check out the details. She left the salary question vague; she didn't ask about the working hours or the living conditions, or even exactly what she would have to do. She never asked to speak to the person who had worked there the previous summer. All she pictured was the chance to ride a horse every day.

Things did not turn out as she had imagined. Her working conditions were wretched, and her salary ended up going for room and board. The worst of it was that her stable duties left her no time to live her dream of horseback riding.

Jesse the violinist, on the other hand, began to check out music prospects early in the school year. He spoke to his school orchestra conductor who sugggested several music camps in addition to some college-sponsored programs. Jesse contacted the camps and college programs and received their information brochures plus the names of some students who had participated in previous years. By sifting through the information and talking to various people, he finally chose a college program that suited his needs and also gave him a chance to experience campus life.

Vivian wanted to see Europe and improve her French. She and her family investigated several possibilities: a teenage bike trip through France; a home exchange sponsored by the American Field Service; a college-endorsed language course in the south of France. After spending considerable time looking into all the prospects, she applied in time for the AFS program.

Rachel wanted to earn some extra money for her senior year. Clerking in a retail store, cashiering in the market, or becoming a receptionist in a doctor's office had little appeal for her. With her distinct interest in botany, Rachel decided to explore the local landscape firms. By working part-time during the busy spring season and gaining experience, she was assured of a good job for the summer.

To sum up, there are four advantages to be gained from planning:

- You will have a number of choices. You don't want to be left with the jobs that are begging for someone because they're dull or poorly paid.
- You will be first in line, so that no one gets the job or internship or place in a program simply by being there ahead of you.
- You will have time to investigate the particulars of your various options.
- If applications are necessary, you will get them in on time.

Looking Forward to Summer

Planning for the summer will give you the great bonus of excitement, something to look forward to. When things seem routine during the school year, knowing that your summer plans are taking shape can spur you on.

Getting the most out of high school includes planning your summers in a creative way. The following list of books and programs will give you some ideas on how to make your summer a very special time.

TIMETABLE FOR SUMMER ACTION

October to December

- Think about your interests
- Read about choices
- Talk over possibilities
- Send for information and applications
- Take notice of deadlines

November to January

- Consult counselor and other adults with relevant experience
- Talk to peers who have done what you're thinking of doing
- Mail applications where required

January to June

Further investigate your preferred options

- Narrow the field of choice
- Make your decision
- Follow through with all necessary preparations

For Your Information

Publications

Billy, Christopher, and John Wells, editors. *Summer Opportunities for Kids and Teenagers.* Princeton, N.J.: Peterson's Guides. Annual.

Council on International Education Exchange. *The Teenager's Guide to Study, Travel, and Adventure Abroad.* New York: St. Martin's Press. Annual.

Eisenberg, Gerson G. *Learning Vacations.* 5th ed. Princeton, N.J.: Peterson's Guides, 1987.

Greenberg, Jan W. J. *The Teenager's Guide to the Best Summer Opportunities.* Cambridge: Harvard Common Press, 1985.

Levin, Shirley. *Summer on Campus: College Experiences for High School Students.* New York: College Entrance Examination Board, 1989.

Organizations

Action, the Federal Domestic Volunteer Agency
Student Community Service Program
806 Connecticut Avenue N.W.
Washington, D.C. 20525

Summer Intern Program
Peace Corps
1990 K Street N.W.
Washington, D.C. 20526

TRIO Programs
U.S. Department of Education
400 Maryland Avenue S.W.
Washington, D.C. 20202

Youth Engaged in Service to America (YES)
The White House
Office of National Service, Room 100
Washington, D.C. 20500

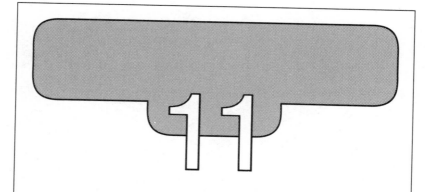

Putting College
in Perspective

Once upon a time in America, you went to college only if you were male, white, and a "gentleman." The earliest colleges were founded to educate future ministers, schoolmasters, and leaders in government and society. As late as 1800, even among those eligible—young white males—only 2 percent went to college.

How times have changed! Today, about 56 percent of all high school graduates enroll in college. Women not only go to college but outnumber men. More than five million students between the ages of 18 and 21 attend a college or university. In total, there are more than 12 million students of all ages enrolled in some form of higher education.

We have in the United States a uniquely diverse higher education system open to people of any race, any religion, any economic background or age. To accommodate this vast and varied population, there are more than 3,000 higher education institutions across the country. These schools are public and private, traditional and innovative, liberal arts and technical. They include junior and community colleges as well as specialized art, drama, and music schools. They can be coed or single sex; historically black or religious in orientation; publicly funded with yearly costs in the low hundreds or privately funded with yearly costs as high as $20,000.

Prospective college students also have a great variety of choice in location, landscape, and size. There are schools right in the neighborhood or thousands of miles away; in the country, the suburbs, small and large cities; on mountaintops, within the sound of the surf. They range in enrollment from under 200 to over 40,000. In other words, there is a place for everyone.

Why Go to College?

Most high school students we've talked to have a practical way of looking at college. They see the college years as their time to prepare for the future. They want a satisfying career, a prestigious occupation, a job that pays well. "College," one student said, "can give my life a better direction."

Practical considerations are good reasons for going to college. But there are many reasons beyond the utilitarian:

- To find out more—about yourself, your world
- To give yourself the chance to change and grow
- To become more independent
- To live in a community of your peers
- To meet people from other geographic, economic, cultural backgrounds
- To learn to think critically and develop your ideas
- To explore an interest in depth
- To be in contact with mentors who can help guide you
- To open up options for further study, career possibilities, and earning power

In addition to expanding your personal horizons, there is a broader reason for going to college. For the early founders of American colleges, the idea was to train special people for leadership so that the new society could survive. Now more than ever, American society needs educated people from all cultures and backgrounds to keep democracy alive and well.

"My father is an elevator mechanic," said one high school student. "That's okay. He makes a good living. But I have great ideas. I want to go into politics, so I can make changes, be a leader. I need to go to college."

Education will greatly increase your chance to be heard and to have an impact on your world.

Seven Wrong Reasons for Counting College Out

1. It's too expensive.

College does take money, but your education may not cost as much as you think. To begin with, publicly supported colleges are far less expensive than privately supported ones. And private colleges that want to attract students of all income levels pledge that no qualified student will be turned away for lack of funds.

Both public and private colleges have developed an aid formula that takes into account your family situation and the cost of college. A financial aid package generally consists of grants, which do not have to be paid back; loans, which you pay back at a low interest rate; and work opportunities on campus for which you are paid. In addition, there are scholarship sources in the outside community.

Financial help is available. Seek out your counselor for initial steps, and see the For Your Information section at the end of this chapter for additional material.

2. Nobody in your family has ever gone.

Once you have expressed an interest in college, you will probably find your family to be supportive. If not, you can help them to understand by explaining all the good reasons you have for wanting to expand your future options. Counselors and teachers will be ready to support and guide you.

3. You won't be able to keep up with the academics.

Many people with mediocre high school records discover that they blossom in the right college. In addition, most colleges offer incoming freshmen programs of study skills, writing workshops, math tutoring, and other academic supports to assist them in making the transition to college. Colleges want you to succeed.

4. You're worried about making new friends.

Nearly everybody worries about that. By the end of the first month, most students have begun to find others with interests in common and to feel at home in their new environment. By the end of your first Thanksgiving holiday, you will probably want to get back to the excitement of campus life.

5. You can get a good job without a college degree.

Recent studies indicate that's just not true. These investigations reveal that college increases job opportunities and earning power. The world is changing very quickly. The kinds of skills many employers are now demanding involve more than straight vocational training. As things stand now, good entry-level jobs often require at least two years of college. Moving up from those jobs requires a higher level of education. People do manage to succeed without a college degree, but it is getting harder and harder to do so. Even those who run the family farm, join the family business, or work at a nonacademic trade find they profit from a college experience.

6. There's too much work involved in applying.

Effective applications *do* take effort, and some take more than others. Applications to state universities, however, are usually easier to deal with than those to private colleges. There are also more than 100 private colleges that have simplified the application process by agreeing to accept a "common application." Some selective colleges have more complicated forms, but once you get the hang of it, filling out the application may help you sort out your personal strengths and objectives.

7. Your grades or scores are not high enough to gain admission.

There is a college for each person who is determined to go. With help from your counselor, you can realistically evaluate your academic and activities record and choose appropriate colleges. The more you learn about the variety of colleges and their selection process, the more options you will discover.

Taking Time Out before College

Going directly on to college from high school as a full-time student is not the right move for everyone. Some students need and benefit from time out. Time out can be a semester or longer. Most high school students think of time out as deferring college for a year. And many colleges encourage taking time out for the right reasons.

One reason to take time out is to build a stronger academic record. If you have been an indifferent student and your college options are limited, or if you are a fair student but your particular college choices are out of reach, you might consider taking some courses at your community college or a junior college, or a fifth year at a prep school. Doing well in these courses will improve your academic credentials and probably expand your options.

Another reason to take time out is to profit more from your college experience once you enroll. Jeannie, for example, had pretty good grades but not much confidence. As she visited colleges, she realized that she didn't know what she liked or didn't like, nor what she wanted or didn't want. Everything about college was one big blur. Jeannie just wasn't ready for this giant step.

For Jeannie and others who are particularly unclear about their aims and uncertain about themselves, time out can be a maturing experience.

Time out, however, is only as good as what you do with it. Time out is not time to hang around. You must have a plan.

One possibility has already been mentioned—courses at a community or junior college, or a fifth year at a prep school. Another option is to explore an area of interest. Neil, for example, wanted to be part of a community project that involved building and urban planning. He volunteered for a year with a service group that was helping rehabilitate houses in a tornado-stricken town.

Instead of working part-time during high school, Leo took a job for a year before entering college. He was able to save up for tuition without sacrificing his high school grades or his place on the soccer team. In his case, he had already applied and been accepted into college, securing a deferred admission from his future alma mater. Most colleges include the option of deferral in their admissions plan.

For a few, travel is a possibility. Almost every high school student would love the chance to travel. If you are lucky enough to be able to plan such a year, make sure it has a good focus. After graduating from high school, Clare spent a year on a kibbutz in Israel, discovering another culture and learning Hebrew.

Aimless traveling, however, just like aimless staying at home, can be disappointing. If you have a purpose, such as learning a language or volunteering for a service project, your time out is more likely to be rewarding.

Perspective on Your College Options

Perspective is the key word as you weigh your college options. What you choose to do, when and where you do it, is affected by many factors besides your academic standing. These factors include your own view of the future, your family situation, the common experience of your community.

In some parts of the country, for instance, college-bound students consider applying only to their state university, where they are almost certain to be accepted. They don't ordinarily explore additional college options.

On the other hand, there are areas of the country in which the whole college process becomes a frantic ordeal. These high school students apply to countless colleges without appraising their appropriateness. The college search is mixed with all kinds of factors like prestige, competition, status. Students face a charged atmosphere of parents' ambitions, competition with peers, and their own sometimes unrealistic expectations. None of this is conducive to calm and rational choice.

Seeing things in perspective means stepping back, looking over the college scene, and figuring out what is best for you. Going to the state university—or to one of a number of state-supported colleges or universities—is fine, provided you have checked it out and found that it meets your requirements. But you may need a smaller school or a more specialized one. You may want the experience of an environment that differs from the one you are used to. You may be overlooking the opportunity to go somewhere outside your immediate area that would suit you better.

On the other hand, the tense, pressured scramble to get into a college with a "name," the anxious concern over whether or not you are qualified—is your class standing high enough, have you participated in the right kind of extracurricular activities, what about those SATs?—can be a waste of energy. When you come right down to it, that name-brand college you are trying to get into may not even be the right place for you.

You must take the time to think about yourself in an organized manner so that you can better match yourself with colleges. Sometimes it is easier to do this with a list of questions in hand. Mull over the following group of questions to gain a clearer idea about yourself and your college choices.

Ten Questions to Help You Put College in Perspective

1. How do you see yourself growing and changing in the next few years? What would be the best environment for that growth?

2. What do you hope to gain from college? What worries you most?

3. Why do you want an education? Why do you want to go to college?

4. Are there any special interests you want to pursue in college? Do your interests require special facilities or programs?

5. At what level of academic challenge do you work best? Do you want a demanding program or one that allows you to do well without knocking yourself out? How do you respond to competition and academic pressure?

6. Do you want to be close to home? Or are you looking forward to exploring a different geographical area?

7. How important are the college surroundings to you? Does it matter whether the college is in a city, a suburb, a small town, or the country?

8. Do you learn best when you set your own pace? Or do you need a structured and directed course of study?

9. How important to you is a close relationship with faculty? Would you prefer the community atmosphere of a small college, or do you crave the greater choice offered by a large university?

10. How is your viewpoint on college affected by pressure from parents, friends, community?

Pressure from Parents

Family tensions reach new heights during college application time. Although some parents stay completely out of the process, others get very involved. Parents are concerned because they recognize that college is an important decision and naturally want what is best for their children.

For some parents, what is "best" equals a "designer-label" school. Name recognition and prestige mean a great deal to them. Other parents expect their children to attend their own alma mater. Still others want their children close to home. Some resist paying for any school not on their "good college" list. And in most families, the high cost of college tuition makes the choice more complicated. As senior year looms ahead, anxiety rises and pressure increases—especially when parents fear that their children won't do the right thing at the right time.

"My parents don't trust me to handle all this college stuff by myself. The more they pester me about what I'm doing, the more I get on edge. Things are really tense in my house," Marge said.

Parents' badgering is not new. A father says to his son:

> Why do you idle about? Go to school . . . recite your assignment, open your schoolbag, write your tablet. . . . Don't stand about in the public square or wander about the boulevard. . . . Go to school, it will be of benefit to you. . . . I, night and day am I tortured because of you. Night and day you waste in pleasures."
>
> —*Smithsonian*, December 1988

Would you believe that this emotional plea comes from a civilization that is more than 5,000 years old? It was carved into a stone tablet by the Sumerians, who were probably the earliest civilization on earth. And what is the proof that they were civilized? Well, they had schools, and they already had parents who were pressuring their children!

There's no way around it. As college application time

draws near, pressure from parents increases, adding to your own anxiety. What can you do about it?

Organization will ease the pressure. The sooner you get organized, the better off you are. But no matter when you start, work through all the phases in the checklist on pages 129–30.

For Your Information

Thinking about College

Boyer, Ernest L. *College: The Undergraduate Experience in America.* New York: Harper and Row, 1987.

The College Board. *The College Handbook.* New York: College Entrance Examination Board. Annual.

Fiske, Edward B. *The Fiske Guide to Colleges.* New York: Times Books, 1989.

Moll, Richard. *The Public Ivys: A Guide to America's Best Public Undergraduate Colleges and Universities.* New York: Viking, 1985.

Munger, Steven. *A Guide to the College Admission Process.* Alexandria, Va.: National Association of College Admission Counselors, 1989.

Schneider, Zola Dincin. *Campus Visits and College Interviews: A Complete Guide for College-Bound Students and Their Families.* New York: College Entrance Examination Board, 1987.

Shields, Charles J. *The College Guide for Parents.* New York: College Entrance Examination Board, 1988.

Yale Daily News, ed. *The Insider's Guide to the Colleges.* New York: St. Martin's Press. Annual.

Financing College

The American Legion. *Need a Lift?* Indianapolis: The American Legion, National Emblem Sales. Annual.

The College Board. *The College Cost Book.* New York: College Entrance Examination Board. Annual.

The College Scholarship Service. *Meeting College Costs.* New York: College Entrance Examination Board. Annual.

Leider, Robert, and Sally Schwab. *The As and Bs of Academic Scholarship.* Alexandria, Va.: Octameron Press. Annual.

U.S. Department of Education. *The Student Guide: Five Federal Financial Aid Programs.* Washington, D.C.: U.S. Government Printing Office, 1989.

Meeting Special Needs

Beckham, Barry, ed. *The Black Student's Guide to College.* New York: E.P. Dutton, 1982.

Crocker, John R. *The Student Guide to Catholic Colleges and Universities.* New York: Harper and Row, 1983.

Cernea, Ruth Fredman, ed. *Jewish Life on Campus.* Washington, D.C.: B'nai B'rith Hillel Foundations, 1989.

Howe, Florence, et al. *Every Woman's Guide to Colleges and Universities.* New York: The Feminist Press of the City University of New York, 1982.

Jarrow, Jane, et al., ed. *How to Choose a College: Guide for the Student with a Disability.* Washington, D.C.: HEATH Resource Center, 1986.

COLLEGE PLANNING PHASES:
A CHECKLIST

Phase 1: Gather Information about Yourself

- *The Academic You*: Your courses, grades, and scores. Make sure your schedule includes SATs, Achievement tests, or ACTs, taken on time.

- *The Personal You:* Your activities in and out of school, including all clubs, volunteer work, travel, hobbies, jobs. Don't neglect your ideals, ambitions, and hopes for the future.

Phase 2: Gather Information about Colleges

- Consult your guidance counselor and college directories for general information.

- Evaluate with your counselor or other college adviser your academic standing and extracurricular activities: the academic you and the personal you.

- Review your responses to the Ten Questions to Help You Put College in Perspective.

- Make a list of colleges to explore, using the advice you've sought out.

- Study course catalogs and college directories for admissions procedures, application deadlines, courses of special interest, campus mood. These books are available in high school and public libraries.

- Attend college conferences at your school and in your area, college fairs, college nights, alumni meetings.

- Look at available college videos.

- Talk to students who are attending college.

COLLEGE PLANNING PHASES (continued)

Phase 3: Organize Your Information

- Refine your college list to a reasonable number.
- Send for applications, financial aid forms, and course catalogs.
- Set up a folder system. You will need to keep track of your applications, deadlines, interviews, and campus visits.

Phase 4: Visit Colleges

- Select colleges to visit.
- Consult some of the books in For Your Information (pages 127–8) for advice on visits and interviews.
- Arrange an itinerary and set up interview appointments and overnights.
- Make visits; take notes.
- Refine college list based on all the information you have gathered.

Phase 5: Apply to College

- Consult For Your Information (pages 127–8) for a list of books on the application process.
- Allow time to reflect, write, and revise essays.
- Fill out applications and financial aid forms. Keep copies for your files.
- Mail applications on time.
- Request recommendations from counselor and teachers.
- Make sure that transcripts and scores are sent to colleges.
- You've done your best. Relax!

From Now On. . .

One student, whom we asked to react to some of the suggestions in this book, said: "I see myself in lots of the situations you talk about. There are ideas in the book I really want to try out. But . . ." she paused. "Excuse me, but there are two things you'll never, ever, catch me doing."

We couldn't wait to hear what they were.

"I will absolutely never get up 15 minutes earlier in the morning. And the last thing in the world I would do is recite French verb conjugations while I swim!"

We laughed and told her she had the right spirit.

This book was never meant to be a set of blueprints, to be followed exactly, as though you were building a house and one mistake would make the roof fall in. Some ideas will seem right for you, others not. This is your chance to take charge, to pick and choose what you will find useful.

In order to take charge and to feel proud of your success you don't have to accomplish everything, or even as much as your best friend. If you learn to shape your experience as you go along, if you practice planning, if you know how to seek help when you need it, if you establish reasonable rules and expectations for yourself, you will create a solid framework for getting the most out of high school. The countdown to college will fit comfortably into that framework.

As you move along, we hope that the elusive idea known as "goal setting"—an idea that parents and teachers talk so much about—will become more natural for you. When you take charge step by step, goals emerge from your everyday experience. You are working toward goals you set for yourself. This steady unfolding of your strengths and values should prove especially helpful as you approach graduation and decisions about college.

Our warmest good wishes go with you!

Index

Advanced Placement (AP) courses, 74–77

Advanced programs, 16–19, 73–80

  Advanced Placement (AP) courses, 74–77

  for developing special talents, 79

  in English, 74–77

  honors courses, 74

  independent study, 78–79

  International Baccalaureate, 77

  internships, 78–79

  lack of, in high school, 77–78

  in languages, 18–19, 74–77

  in mathematics, 16–17, 74–77

  in science, 17–18, 74–77

After-school activities. *See* Extracurricular activities

Alcoholism, 88, 89, 92

Algebra, 17

Anxiety, math, 17

Arts

  Advanced Placement courses in, 74–77

  in college preparatory programs, 15

Assignment book, 49

Assignments. *See* Homework

Athletics, 96, 98–99

Balance, in academic schedule, 19–20

Basic courses

  examples of, 14

  importance of, 13–14

  moving beyond, 14–15

  scheduling of, 19–20

Book reviews, 26–27

Books. *See* Reading

Boredom

  listening and, 54–56

  reading versus, 24

Boyer, Ernest L., 23

Calculus, 16–17

Classroom

  asking questions in, 31–33

  note taking in, 57–59

  seating position in, 55, 56

Club advisers, as troubleshooters, 68

Coaches, as troubleshooters, 68

College admissions counselors, 75

College admissions tests, 24

College-level courses

  Advanced Placement (AP), 74–77

  at community colleges, 77–79, 122–123

  International Baccalaureate, 77

College planning, 119–128
  checklist for, 127–128
  options in, 124–125
  parental pressure and, 125–126
  reasons for attending college, 119–120
  reasons for not attending college, 120–122
  taking time out before college, 122–123
  types of colleges, 119
College preparatory program
  additional courses in, 14–15
  analysis of high school curriculum and, 19
  basic courses in, 13–15, 19–20
  heavy schedule in, 19
  outstanding courses of school and, 16
  scheduling of, 19–20
Communication skills. See Listening; Reading; Speaking; Writing
Community colleges, 77–79, 122–123
Community organizations, 89–90, 99–100, 110, 123
Conferences, benefitting from, 69
Content, of courses, 15
Correspondence courses, 78
Cramming, 24

Deadlines, 44–46
Death in family, 91
Debate team, 32
Decision making, 9
Desk, organization of, 47–48
Dillon, Dorothy H., 75
Divorce, 91
Drama club, 32, 95

Elective courses
  outstanding courses of school as, 16
  quality and content of, 15
  scheduling of, 16, 19–20
English
  Advanced Placement courses in, 74–77
  in college preparatory program, 14, 15
Escalante, Jaime, 37
Extracurricular activities, 38, 41, 95–104
  advantages of, 96–97
  checklist of potential, 103
  examples of, 95–96, 97–99
  maintaining reasonable participation in, 97–99
  paid part-time work, 86–87, 100–102, 111
  volunteer work, 99–100, 110, 123

Family
  dealing with problems in, 87–92
  move to a new area by, 83–86, 92
  need for part-time work and, 86–87, 101–102
  See also Parents
Financial aid, 121
Foreign languages. See Languages
Forensics society, 32
Friends
  in college, 121
  moving to another school and, 83–86
  as troubleshooters, 68

Gilbar, Steven, 25–26
Goals, 8, 9
Good Books (Gilbar), 25–26
Grades
    Advanced Placement courses
        and, 74–77
    college admission and, 122
    extracurricular activities and,
        96–97
Guidance counselors, 14
    college planning and, 121
    moving to a new school and,
        85
    as troubleshooters, 67–70, 88–
        89

Hearing, listening versus, 53–54
Homework, 41
    organization of, 48–49
    organization of work area for,
        47–48
    procrastination and, 43–47
Honors courses, 74
Hotlines, 90

Illness in family, 91
Imagination, boredom and, 55–
    56
Independent study, 78–79
International Baccalaureate, 77
Internships, 78–79
Interviews, speaking skills and,
    31

Journal writing, 29

Languages
    advanced courses in, 18–19,
        74–77
    in college preparatory pro-
        grams, 15

International Baccalaureate
    and, 77
Letter writing, 29
Librarians, as troubleshooters,
    68
Library
    browsing through, 25–26
    importance of, 23
    information on family prob-
        lems from, 89–92
Listening, 53–59
    avoiding distractions in, 56
    boredom and, 54–56
    hearing versus, 53–54
    note taking and, 57–59
    tips for, 56

Magazines, 26
    book reviews in, 26–27
Magnet schools, 79
Mathematics
    advanced courses in, 16–17,
        74–77
    in college preparatory pro-
        gram, 14, 15
    International Baccalaureate
        and, 77
Mistakes, 9
Movies, 24–25
Moving to a new school, 83–86,
    92
    leaving process, 84–85
    settling-in process, 85–86

National Endowment for the Hu-
    manities Young Scholars
    Program, 79
Newspapers
    book reviews in, 26–27
    school, 95–96
Notebook, organization of, 48–49

Note taking, 57–59
  in classroom, 57–59
  reviewing notes and, 59
  tips for, 57

Office supplies, 47–48
Organization
  of notebook and assignments, 48–49
  of time, 37–47
  of work area, 47–48
Orientations, 14

Parents
  college planning and, 125–126
  procrastination and, 46–47
  as troubleshooters, 68, 88–89
  See also Family
Parents of friends, as trouble-shooters, 68, 88–89
Part-time work, 100–102
  advantages of, 100–101
  choices of, 102
  family need for, 86–87, 101–102
  summer jobs, 111
Persistence in solving problems, 69–70
Physics, advanced courses in, 17–18
Planning
  for college, 19–20, 119–128
  for summer vacations, 112–115
  See also Scheduling; Time management
Problem solving, 65–70
  benefitting from conferences, 69
  common excuses for resisting help, 67
  examples of need for, 65–67

family issues, 87–92
information sources for, 89–92
moving to a new school, 83–86, 92
need for paid work, 86–87, 101–102
people who can help with, 67–69, 88–91
persistence in, 69–70
Procrastination, 43–47
  as consistent problem, 43–45
  parental pressure and, 46–47
  reasons for, 45
  stopping, 46

Quality, of courses, 15
Questions
  in classroom, 31–33
  from classroom notes, 59
  in textbook study process, 60–61

Reading, 23–28, 43
  book reviews and, 26–27
  browsing through library, 25–26
  discovering books and, 23
  finding time for, 27–28
  information on family problems and, 89–92
  movies and television versus, 24–25
  rewards of, 24
  sources of books, 25–26
  in textbook study, 59–61
  tips for, 27
Reciting, in textbook study process, 61
Relatives
  as troubleshooters, 68, 88–89
  See also Family; Parents

Religious leaders, as trouble-
  shooters, 68, 88–89
Required courses. *See* Basic
  courses
Responsibility, 7–8
Review
  of classroom notes, 59
  in textbook study process, 61
Risk taking, 8, 9
Robinson, Francis P., 60

Scheduling
  of basic courses, 19–20
  of elective courses, 16, 19–20
  time chart in, 39–43
  time to read and, 27–28
  See also Planning; Time man-
    agement
Scholastic Aptitude Tests (SATs),
  24
School newspaper, 95–96
Science
  advanced courses in, 17–18,
    74–77
  in college preparatory pro-
    gram, 14, 15
  developing special talent in, 79
  International Baccalaureate
    and, 77
Seating, classroom, 55, 56
Selective colleges
  academic requirements for,
    14–15
  advanced courses and, 16–19,
    74–77
  International Baccalaureate
    and, 77
Self-confidence, and speaking
  skills, 30–33
Self-evaluation, 8, 32–33
Social activities, 41

Social studies
  Advanced Placement courses
    in, 74–77
  in college preparatory pro-
    gram, 14, 15
  International Baccalaureate
    and, 77
Speaking, 30–33
  asking questions and, 31–33
  importance of, 30–31
  tips for, 32
Sports, 96, 98–99
S Q 3R method, 60–61
Stand and Deliver (film), 37
Study skills, 59–62
  checklist for, 62
  S Q 3R method, 60–61
Substance abuse, 88, 89, 92
Suicide, 90, 92
Summer jobs, 111
Summer programs, 18–19
Summer vacations, 107–116
  for experience beyond class-
    room, 107–108
  flexible approach to, 112
  fulfilling wishes for, 110–111
  planning for, 112–115
  practical considerations for,
    111
  wish list for, 108–109
Supplies, work area, 47–48
Survey, in textbook study pro-
  cess, 60

Teachers
  boredom and, 54–56
  college planning and, 121
  moving to a new school and,
    85
  questions from students and,
    31, 32

Teachers *(continued)*
  as troubleshooters, 67–70, 88–89
Telephone calls, 38, 41
Telephone hotlines, 90
Television, 24–25, 38, 41
Textbook, study skills for using, 59–61
Time management, 37–49
  organization of notebook and assignments, 48–49
  organization of work area, 47–48
  procrastination in, 43–47
  time chart in, 39–43
  time wasters and, 38–40
  See also Planning; Scheduling
Time out before college, 122–123
Travel, 111, 123
Troubleshooting, 65–70
  benefitting from conferences, 69
  common excuses for resisting help, 67
  examples of need for, 65–67, 83–88
  people who can help in, 67–69, 88–91
  persistence in, 69–70
Tutors, as troubleshooters, 68

Vacations. *See* Summer vacations
Vocabulary, 24
  in textbook study process, 61
Volunteer work, 99–100, 110, 123

Westinghouse Science Search, 79
Work area, organization of, 47–48
Writing, 28–30
  importance of, 28
  practice in, 29–30
  tips for, 29

Other Books of Interest from the College Board

Item Number

003179   *Campus Health Guide*, by Carol L. Otis, M.D., and Roger Goldingay. A comprehensive medical guide, written expressly for college students, that stresses the link between a healthy lifestyle and a productive college experience. ISBN: 0-87447-317-9, $14.95

002601   *Campus Vistis and College Interviews*, by Zola Dincin Schneider. An "insider's" guide to campus visits and college interviews, including 12 checklists that will help students make the most of these firsthand opportunities. ISBN: 0-87447-260-1, $9.95

002261   *The College Admissions Organizer.* This unique planning tool for college-bound students includes inserts and fill-in forms, plus 12 large pockets to store important admissions materials. ISBN: 0-87447-226-1, $16.95

002687   *The College Board Achievement Tests.* Complete and actual Achievement Tests given in 13 subjects, plus the College Board's official advice on taking the tests. ISBN: 0-87447-268-7, $9.95

003101   *The College Board Guide to Preparing for the PSAT/NMSQT.* Contains four actual tests as well as practical test-taking tips, sample questions, and a comprehensive math review section. ISBN: 0-87447-310-1, $8.95

002938   *The College Board Guide to the CLEP Examinations.* Contains nearly 900 questions from CLEP general and subject examinations, plus other information. ISBN: 0-87447-293-8, $8.95

003047   *College Bound: The Student's Handbook for Getting Ready, Moving In, and Succeeding on Campus*, by Evelyn Kaye and Janet Gardner. Help for high school seniors as they face the responsibilities and independence of being college freshmen. ISBN: 0-87447-304-7, $9.95

003152   *The College Cost Book, 1988–89.* A step-by-step guide to 1988–89 college costs and detailed financial aid for 3,100 accredited institutions. ISBN: 0-87447-315-2, $12.95 (Updated annually)

003160   *The College Guide for Parents*, by Charles J. Shields. Useful information on such topics as college choice, standardized testing, college applications, financial aid, and coping with separation anxiety. ISBN: 0-87447-316-0, $12.95

003136   *The College Handbook, 1988–89.* The College Board's official directory to more than 3,100 two- and four-year colleges and universities. ISBN: 0-87447-313-6, $16.95 (Updated annually)

002490   *College to Career*, by Joyce Slayton Mitchell. A guide to more than 100 careers, telling what the work is like, the education and personal skills needed, how many people are employed, where they work, and starting salaries and future employment prospects. ISBN: 0-87447-249-0, $9.95.

003055   *How to Help Your Teenager Find the Right Career*, by Charles J. Shields. Step-by-step advice and innovative ideas to help parents motivate their children to explore careers and find alternatives suited to their interests and abilities. ISBN: 0-87447-305-5, $12.95

002482   *How to Pay for Your Children's College Education*, by Gerald Krefetz. Practical advice to help parents of high school students, as well as of young children, finance their children's college education. ISBN: 0-87447-248-2, $12.95

003144   *Index of Majors, 1988–89*. Lists 500 majors at the 3,000 colleges and graduate institutions, state by state, that offer them. ISBN: 0-87447-314-4, $13.95 (Updated annually)

002911   *Profiles in Achievement*, by Charles M. Holloway. Traces the careers of eight outstanding men and women who used education as the key to later success. (Hardcover, ISBN: 0-87447-291-1, $15.95); 002857 paperback (ISBN: 0-87447-285-7, $9.95)

002598   *Succeed with Math*, by Sheila Tobias. A *practical* guide that helps students overcome math anxiety and gives them the tools for mastering the subject in high school and college courses as well as the world of work. ISBN: 0-87447-259-8, $12.95

003225   *Summer on Campus*, by Shirley Levin. A comprehensive guide to more than 250 summer programs at over 150 universities. ISBN: 0-87447-322-5, $9.95

003039   *10 SATs: Third Edition*. Ten actual, recently administered SATs plus the full text of *Taking the SAT*, the College Board's official advice. ISBN: 0-87447-303-9, $9.95

002571   *Writing Your College Application Essay*, by Sarah Myers McGinty. An informative and reassuring book that helps students write distinctive application essays and explains what colleges are looking for in these essays. ISBN: 0-87447-257-1, $9.95

002474   *Your College Application*, by Scott Gelband, Catherine Kubale, and Eric Schorr. A step-by-step guide to help students do their best on college applications. ISBN: 0-87447-247-4, $9.95

To order by direct mail any books not available in your local bookstore, please specify the item number and send your request with a check made payable to the College Board for the full amount to: College Board Publications, Department M53, Box 886, New York, New York 10101-0886. Allow 30 days for delivery. An institutional purchase order is required in order to be billed, and postage will be charged on all billed orders. Telephone orders are not accepted, but information regarding any of the above titles is available by calling Publications Customer Service at (212) 713-8165.